Contents

Acknowledgments v

Introduction 1

1 Congratulations! You're Normal 5
2 The Music Career Advising Puzzle 13
3 All About You 25
4 Music Career Trends 39
5 Bachelor of Music in Performance 47
6 Bachelor of Music in Music Theory 55
7 Bachelor of Music in Composition 61
8 Bachelor of Music in Music History and Literature 67
9 Bachelor of Music in Sacred Music 73
10 Bachelor of Music in Jazz Studies 79
11 Bachelor of Music in Pedagogy 85
12 Bachelor of Music in Musical Theater 93
13 Bachelor of Music in Music Business/Industry 99
14 Bachelor of Music in Electrical Engineering/Recording Technology 109
15 Bachelor of Music in Music Therapy 117
16 Bachelor of Music in Music Education 123
17 Music Librarian 131
18 Conducting 139
19 Instrument Repair 147

Annotated Bibliography 153
About the Author 163

Acknowledgments

This book is dedicated to my wife, Devyn, and to my daughters, Hope and Meg; with special appreciation to Warren Henry, Darhyl Ramsey, and Debbie Rohwer. Finally, I would like to acknowledge the music students and parents of student musicians whose questions served as the inspiration for this book and the professional musicians whose answers made it possible.

Introduction

This book was inspired by a simple question that has been asked by music students and parents of student musicians for generations: What can I really do with a music degree?

I first heard this question when I began teaching at the college level and served as an academic advisor to the music education majors at my university. I also observed that a lot of students selected degree programs that did not seem to suit their skills and interests, that were of little interest to them, or that did not lead to any viable career options. Finally, I noticed that music students seemed to change majors more often than their colleagues in different programs.

As I began talking more frequently with students about their career choices, I came to two realizations. First, a lot of music students choose to major in a particular field because they are unaware of the full range of music career possibilities. Simply stated, they choose a degree because it is the most appealing of what they perceive as the extent of their options, even though they may not be particularly interested in their chosen field.

The second observation is directly linked to the first. Students who choose a degree as a lesser of two evils are less likely to consider whether or not they are really a good fit in their chosen career paths. A music student who is aware only of careers in performance and music education, for example, may choose a performance degree because he or she does not want to teach, failing to account for the skills, abilities, and other traits that are essential for a successful career as a performing musician.

As I began some initial research into the world of music careers, I came to the conclusion that the observations I made of my music students were not unique to my university. In truth, there is a great deal of research suggesting that the music career field is a great mystery, especially to student musicians and their parents. I was also reminded of my own, indirect path into a career as a music educator, and I was humbled by the reality that I had experienced the same career questions and concerns when I was a college student.

Similarly, many of my current colleagues and other professional acquaintances have shared their own misguided attempts to select an undergraduate degree as students. Recognizing these traits in myself, in my colleagues, and in my students helped me understand that these commonalities are not unique to any particular type of student, or any particular generation, gender, or other descriptor. They are the reality in

1

which students struggle as they transition from high school to college and from college to career.

These observations and the questions posed by my music students eventually developed into a formal research study whose results are presented in this book. The purpose of this study was to identify the extent of music career options, and to identify the skills, interests, work values, and personal attributes that will help students determine their suitability for a career in music. Given that this was a formal research study, there were official procedures that were followed and protocol that was observed. As this book is not a formal research report, I will not disclose the extent of that information herein.

I do feel it is important, however, to explain a few of the specifics of this study, primarily to establish the validity and credibility of its contents. First, the career advising procedures suggested in this book coincide with established guidelines recommended by academic advisors and career advisors in universities and in the public market. Similarly, the content of each chapter was obtained in a manner that coincides with these guidelines and that abides by standard research protocol.

Next, the music career information included in this book was obtained through formal interviews with approximately 100 university music faculty members and professional musicians in each of the represented career fields. Prior to selecting potential interviewees, specific criteria were set to ensure that each interviewed musician was a well-established professional with a successful track record, marked by achievement.

Finally, this book has been organized using the undergraduate Bachelor of Music degree titles as a system of music career categorization. Each chapter's title is taken from one of the twelve undergraduate music degrees offered by colleges around the country, and each chapter inventories the careers that are related to the corresponding degree. The intent of this grouping is to direct students to the most appropriate college degree based on specific career goals.

As of this writing, there are twelve accredited undergraduate music degrees, or Bachelor of Music degrees. These degrees are:

- Bachelor of Music in Performance
- Bachelor of Music in Music Theory
- Bachelor of Music in Composition
- Bachelor of Music in Music History and Literature
- Bachelor of Music in Sacred Music
- Bachelor of Music in Jazz Studies
- Bachelor of Music in Pedagogy
- Bachelor of Music in Musical Theatre
- Bachelor of Music in Music Business/Industry
- Bachelor of Music with Studies in Electrical Engineering and/or Recording Technology

- Bachelor of Music in Music Therapy
- Bachelor of Music in Music Education

Before continuing further, there are two points of clarification to make concerning the degrees and careers included in this book. First, it is common to find some variation among universities concerning the names of the degrees offered by their music departments. As an example, some universities title their sacred music degree a Bachelor of Music in Church Music rather than using the term *sacred* music. Although this is a minute point, it may cause confusion among some who look for specific degree titles rather than degree fields.

Second, the final three chapters of this book describe music career fields that are not currently affiliated with a specific Bachelor of Music degree: music librarian, conductor, and music instrument repair technician. Although there is not currently a degree title associated with these careers, there are many viable career options in each field, and there are many degree programs that adequately prepare students to enter these fields. Each chapter contains specific information regarding career entry and required training for the related career field.

HOW TO USE THIS BOOK

This book has been divided into three sections. The first section provides a generalized overview of career advising procedures and of the types of information to explore as the reader considers a career in music. The final chapters of this section also present music career information that is generalizable or applicable to a majority of music career fields. This information includes trends and job requirements that are applicable to a majority of music careers, as well as the personality traits that may be desirable for professional musicians in any music career.

The second section of this book transitions from general to specific with regard to career descriptions and related information. Each chapter lists the careers that are available in the related field and provides a basic description of the available careers. Each chapter also lists and describes the skills, interests, work values, and personal characteristics that professional musicians and university faculty members reported as necessary attributes for compatibility in their respective fields.

Each chapter has been organized into the following sections:

- General description of the career field
- Important steps for career entry (may not be applicable to all fields)
- Inventory and general description of the jobs available in the related field
- Most promising geographic locations for jobs in the related field

- What it takes to be a good fit:
    - An inventory of the musical and nonmusical skills needed in the field
    - An inventory of the musical and nonmusical interests that typically lead people to pursue a career in the related field
    - An inventory of the musical and nonmusical work values, or how people typically feel rewarded in the field
    - An inventory of the personality characteristics and other traits that may determine compatibility in the field

This book concludes with an annotated bibliography of additional music career books, websites, and other resources. While the purpose of this book is to serve as an introduction to music careers as a whole, many of the resources in the annotated bibliography are devoted to a very narrow range of music careers and will therefore provide more detailed, career-specific information.

Because it is easier to update a website than a book, the websites included in the bibliography may contain the most up-to-date information concerning salaries, the number of available jobs, and other information that may become out of date more quickly in books. Many websites, however, are not created by musicians and may present an erroneous or incomplete inventory of music careers in any given field.

As a disclaimer, this book is not intended as an endorsement of any college program, music career book, website, or other publication, or as a critique of the resources included in the bibliography. The purpose of including them in this book is to help the reader find additional information about specific areas of music study, written by professionals in those fields with the qualifications to write career-specific texts.

CLOSING THOUGHTS

As a final detail, participants in formal research projects are typically promised complete and total anonymity. Therefore, the names of the professional musicians and university faculty members who were interviewed for this book will not be disclosed. Although I cannot reveal their names, I would like to conclude this introduction with a word of gratitude to all the musicians who participated in the interviews that led to this book. It is my sincerest hope that your words of wisdom will guide future music students into careers that will bring them lifelong fulfillment and satisfaction.

ONE

Congratulations! You're Normal

As you enter your last year of high school and first years of college, you will be faced with a number of exciting, albeit frightening decisions that directly impact the next two to forty-two years of your life. If they have not already started, your friends, parents, and teachers may soon begin asking you which college you want to attend, what course of study you intend to pursue, what you plan to do when you graduate, and many other questions about your future.

Once you begin telling people about your final plans, you will undoubtedly be flooded with an array of feedback, both opposing and supporting your decisions. For music students, the diversity of opinions regarding your potential to succeed in a music career may seem more exaggerated when compared to other career fields.

Nonmusical parents or teachers, for example, may call your attention to the large number of street musicians performing on corners and sidewalks, begging for tips. Or, they may tell you of the countless number of their acquaintances who took an entry-level job in a factory, waiting for years for their big break into the music industry. They may also ask you to consider the millions of *American Idol* contestants who left the stage in tears after their dreams of a music career were crushed. If you are lucky, you will be surrounded by people who support your decision to pursue a career in music and who will work to help you find answers to your questions about music careers.

In either case, however, you may find that there is a relatively small number of people with adequate knowledge, experience, and insight into music careers. Parents without musical training may feel at a complete loss when faced with questions about music careers. Music teachers may have extensive experience in education or performance but may not be aware of some of the less-common music career fields and may therefore feel equally unprepared to answer your questions. Even professional musicians state that they are unaware of many music career possibilities outside of their individual fields. Given these factors, it is only natural if you feel perplexed in your music degree and career decisions.

If you are a student musician considering the possibility of music as a career, feeling somewhat overwhelmed by the enormity of your decision, and torn between the constant stream of conflicting advice from friends, teachers, and parents, congratulations, you're normal. If you are the parent or guardian of a student musician, concerned that your child may be investing his or her time and energy into an unprofitable career, and wishing that he or she would at least consider other options, congratulations, you're normal. If you are the teacher or advisor of a student musician, trapped between parents' wishes that their child enter a lucrative career and the student's desire to feel artistically and professionally fulfilled in his or her future work, congratulations, you're normal.

TO MUSIC STUDENTS

While you may feel that your particular background, musical experiences, or other traits set you apart from other student musicians, know that there are many music students who share your fears as you take the next precautious steps toward a possible career in music. Specifically, there are three worries that are common among student musicians who are considering a music career: ignorance, indecisiveness, and impressionability. A simple awareness of these concerns will not lessen their impact, but it will help you to cope with the snares that typically trick students into making the wrong choices or making decisions for the wrong reasons.

Ignorance

First, you may feel somewhat uninformed, or perhaps outright ignorant concerning career options, particularly in music. For most high school students, your primary participation with music is through performance, so you are naturally aware of careers in performance. You have also worked with at least one professional music educator who most likely encouraged you to consider music as a career, so you know a lot about the possibility of becoming a music teacher. You may have also been exposed to a smattering of other types of music careers but may not know enough about them to consider them as viable music career options.

Based on this limited selection of options, many student musicians choose nonmusical career fields because they do not feel that they are good enough as singers or instrumentalists to succeed as performers, nor do they want to teach music. If you feel yourself trapped in this situation, you should know that there are numerous music career possibilities in addition to performance and education that will be explored in later chapters of this book.

In the meantime, however, there is one more aspect of ignorance revealed in this scenario. In addition to a limited knowledge of music career options, you may feel like you do not know what it will take to be successful in your chosen music career. Based on the limited view of music career options, many first-year music students elect to major in performance because they do not want to teach or choose education because they do not feel like they are strong enough performers.

In reality, a lack of performance ability does not mean you will be a good music educator, and not wanting to teach does not mean you should major in performance. More so, each music career requires a unique combination of skills, abilities, and other attributes that will help you determine your potential for success. In addition to providing information about music career options, this book will help you identify key attributes about yourself, both as a musician and as an individual, that will help you determine this potential.

Indecisiveness

Next, you may feel like you vacillate back and forth between two or more music career options, and that it is hard to make a final decision. Sometimes, initial career decisions are rash or impulsive, based on reactions and emotions rather than on logic and reasoning. Sometimes, plans change once you get to college and begin to identify professional interests in an area you had not previously considered. Other times, the appearance of indecisiveness simply stems from the process of weighing your options before making a final decision.

As an example, most music degrees require freshmen to take introductory-level theory classes. As many high school music programs do not offer theory, you may have never experienced this aspect of music and may become frustrated by your lack of knowledge when you begin college. These feelings may cause you to believe that you are incapable or should no longer pursue music as a career.

Or, more commonly, your first career decisions may be based solely on interest or first impressions. As you talk with people about this decision, you may learn more about the career that causes you to change your mind. As you continue to seek input from teachers, friends, classmates, and parents, new ideas and opinions may lead you in an entirely different direction.

For whatever the reason, there are a lot of factors that may cause you to question your decisions. As this happens, you may very well be tempted to change majors from one music career field to another, or to a degree that is completely unrelated to music. While this may make you appear fickle or uncertain, it is a natural process that must occur to ensure you make the best college and career decisions.

Impressionability

Lastly, you may feel that every bit of information you read or every piece of advice you receive about music careers causes you to question your decisions. This is especially likely when advice from a parent conflicts with input from a teacher or friend. These conflicting opinions may cause you to vacillate between two or more options, or to suddenly choose a route that you had not previously considered. As you wade through the sea of input and advice, listen respectfully while cautiously filtering through advice from people who may not be qualified to give it. In short, consider the source.

Music, as a career field, possesses a number of unique characteristics that complicate the usual process of seeking career advice from friends, teachers, and family. Specifically, there may be a skewed view of reality concerning music careers among students considering a career in music, and among friends or adults attempting to give career advice.

First, the recent popularity of music reality shows and other music-related television programs may have generated the appearance that anyone can be successful as a musician, and that success comes easily. However, the reality, particularly in performance-based careers, is that success is not defined by fame, and it comes only to a select few who are adamantly dedicated to music.

Next, a large portion of the population was at one time involved in a musical activity of some kind, whether singing in a children's choir at school or a place of worship, taking piano lessons, or playing an instrument in beginning band. Even those with no musical background attend concerts, listen to the radio, or in some other way profess a deep connection to music. As a result, there many people who feel qualified to provide input concerning music careers, claiming their own background or interest as credentials.

In addition, although family, friends, and teachers are well intentioned, their input can be easily tainted by a number of factors. First, the people closest to you are commonly biased in your favor and may not be able to provide the most objective evaluation of your abilities or of your potential for success. This may directly influence the type of advice they provide when you ask them for input regarding your music career decisions.

Next, because many people have prior experiences in music, you can assume that there are a lot of people who have failed in their own attempts at a music career. These attempts may range from people who tried for a semester or two in college to major in music, to people who may have auditioned for major symphonies and opera houses, or perhaps even maintained a fairly successful yet short-lived musical career. From their own experiences, then, it is likely that these people will suggest that music should be pursued only as a hobby, or that you will never be successful as a musician.

A final concern is that input provided by one group of people may be in direct contrast to information provided by others. Fact-based advice from a band or choir director, for example, may be in direct conflict with opinion-based input from a friend or colleague. Yes, you need to hear a variety of opinions, but this can quickly become too much of a good thing, especially when one group's advice contradicts suggestions from other sources, and when input is sought from people who are not qualified to give it.

Self-Realization

As you read, and perhaps reread through the information described previously, I challenge you to honestly assess the extent to which each trait applies to you. If you find that you closely associate with one or more of these descriptions, congratulations, you're normal. As you read, also remember that sometime an honest self-assessment can be painful. I suggest that it would be more painful for you to make a wrong decision now and regret it in the future than to allow brutal honesty to accurately guide your career decisions. Therefore, as you read:

Be patient. You have time. It is common for students to enter college with only a vague idea of what they might want to do as a career, or to have no idea at all. It is also common, although not as desirable, for students to change their minds after graduating from college. Ideally, your first few years of college will answer the lingering questions you may have about a music career.

Be open-minded. Be willing to pursue options that were not your original intent. Be willing to explore, and participate in music-related activities that may not initially interest you. In doing so, you may find your niche in an area you had not previously considered.

Be industrious. Spend extra time and energy to learn as much as you can about yourself, about music, and about the full extent of music career possibilities.

Be inquisitive. Seek the input of professionals in the field, of people who have succeeded in music and can be objective judges of your abilities and who can comment without prejudice on your potential for success in a music career.

Be discerning. Take heed of uninformed or inaccurate advice that may cause you to make the wrong career choices. Likewise, be cautious of opinion-based input, or input from people who may be biased one way or another. Your girlfriend or boyfriend, for example, may not be the most suitable person to assess your abilities. Similarly, a person who tells you that you will not make it as a musician because he or she was unsuccessful may not be the best source of input.

Be humble. Recognize that you have a lot to learn even though you may feel like you know everything you need. It has been said that is impossible to teach people who already think they know everything.

TO PARENTS AND GUARDIANS OF MUSIC STUDENTS

If your own lack of knowledge leaves you feeling somewhat apprehensive about answering your student's music career questions, congratulations, you're normal. If you inwardly support your student's intentions to pursue music as a career, but withhold your input feeling that your bias may cloud your advice, you, too, are normal.

Music career research indicates that students commonly make career choices as a direct result of their parents' advice. Parents take students to their first piano lessons. They hear the first blats, squawks, squeaks, and honks in the first lessons, and they hear the well-rehearsed melodies at the senior recital. Parents are rightfully proud of their student's accomplishments and feel that there may be no more suitable career field for their child than music.

Just as students commonly make decisions because of parental advice, some may also make decisions in spite of parental input. For example, when a parent who failed at his or her own attempt at a music career advises a student against a career in music, the student may become more determined to succeed in music. The student's "just because they failed does not mean that I will" mind-set becomes a powerful motivator to succeed against all odds.

Similarly, when parents with no formal music training try to provide advice pertaining to music careers, students propose, "They have no idea what they're talking about," and pursue a music career against parental advice. Finally, well-informed, musical parents may recognize a musical deficiency in their students and advise against a pursuit of a career in music. Regardless, the student sets out with an "I'll show them that I can do it, anyway" attitude, sometimes with a more dogged determination than before.

Parents: as you are aware, you are a vitally important part of helping your student make appropriate and informed career choices, musical or otherwise. Do not allow your role as a parent to cloud your opinion of your child's abilities when offering career advice. You have seen your child progress from a beginner to an advanced musician, but this does not necessarily indicate that he or she possesses the required talents and other traits to be a professional musician. Second, do not allow your own experiences, or lack thereof, to impact your advice. Despite your possibly negative experiences, your student may just be good enough to succeed.

If you do not feel knowledgeable enough to answer your student's questions, do not hesitate to contact a music teacher at your student's school. You may also contact a local university music department and ask to speak with an advisor. If knowledge is power, as the old adage holds, then your increased knowledge will not only empower you to answer your student's questions, but may also ease some fears you may have about advising your student toward a career in music.

TO MUSIC TEACHERS AND ADVISORS OF MUSIC STUDENTS

I challenge you especially to consider the value of your input. To most students, you are the musical expert, whether you feel this way or not. You may view your role as *only* the private instructor, ensemble director, or theory tutor, and you may feel ill equipped to provide career advice. Regardless, your students will seek you out regarding their music career questions, and they will take your input as solid, irrefutable truth. While parents have a strong impact on career decisions, research indicates that music teachers have a more direct impact on students' music career decisions. Therefore, your role in the decision-making process is one of extreme importance.

You owe it to your students and to yourself to become and remain cognizant and fully aware of the fullest extent of music career options and resources. This does not, however, imply that you should feel compelled to provide input where you are not qualified to give it. If you do not know enough, or feel that you are not the right person to provide an objective, informed opinion, there are several options for you to consider.

There are numerous music career resources that are available online and in your local library and bookstore. The final section of this book contains an annotated bibliography of music career resources that may be of assistance. You may also invite professional musicians in a variety of career fields to provide guest lectures in your ensembles or general music classes. You may also help your students contact professionals in a variety of music fields who can provide more objective, knowledgeable insight into your students' areas of interest.

CONCLUSION

There are a lot of unknowns in the process of making career decisions in music. Students commonly feel ignorant, indecisive, and impressionable as they wade through the sea of advice and input from parents, teachers, friends, and anyone else willing to comment. Likewise, parents and teachers may feel ill informed, or in many other ways incapable of pro-

viding music career advice. While this book may not answer all your
questions, it will hopefully point you in the right direction as you seek to
cure the ignorance and take the first steps toward a well-informed decision.

TWO

The Music Career Advising Puzzle

As you weigh your options and consider whether a career in music is the best choice for you, you will no doubt be flooded with a range of questions about career options, job descriptions, income potential, and the likelihood of finding a job. While these job-related questions are crucial, you will also need to consider questions about you: your skills, interests, and other attributes that will help you determine whether or not you will be a good fit in your chosen career.

This chapter describes essential career-related questions you should ask about yourself and about music career possibilities as you consider your career options. As you answer these questions, you will be led through the process of combining essential pieces of information in the right order to help you make adequate and informed career decisions. This chapter also describes several common pitfalls of jumping into a career without adequate or accurate information, and the results of making hasty, uninformed career decisions.

LOOK BEFORE YOU LEAP

The first step in the process of making a large financial investment is to conduct thorough research on the product you wish to purchase. The process of choosing a career is no different, except that in this case, the product is you. In choosing a career path and the degree that will lead you to that career, you are making a significant investment of time, energy, and money in your future. Making hasty, uninformed decisions about your future often leads to wasted money and time in college as you flounder from one degree program to the next, desperately searching for the area where you might be most successful.

A thoughtful and purposeful approach to your career goals, however, may move you more expediently through the training process and into the career field. This is especially vital in the initial steps of the research process. It is helpful, then, to begin with a proper perspective into training to become a professional musician. This perspective will guide you along the way, help you understand certain aspects of becoming a professional musician, and identify how each aspect applies to your particular music career goals.

The College Music Experience

If you feel that a career in music is the most suitable path for you, you will obviously major in one of the music degrees that are described later in this book. The first thing you should know about majoring in music at the college level is that it will most likely feel significantly different from your high school musical experiences.

In most high schools, participation in music simply means performing in one or more large ensembles, competing in solo and ensemble contests, and possibly taking private lessons. A lucky few also take high school music theory classes and perhaps an introduction to music history. College-level music programs, however, involve a significantly deeper academic and theoretical study of music, in addition to a rigorous performance requirement.

As a result, it is common for first-year music majors to change their career goals, stating that they enjoyed participating in music in high school, but do not enjoy the extensive study and practice required at the college level. Some students state that the rigorous requirements make them feel as though they have lost their passion for music. For students who express this sentiment, it may be the case that music is a better avocational pursuit (hobby) rather than a professional interest.

Therefore, consider your own level of music enjoyment as a primary factor of suitability for a career in music. If extensive academic and analytical study of music ruins your joy of participating in musical activities, you may be better suited to a career that is less contingent on your musical knowledge and ability. If, however, you feel a sense of personal and musical satisfaction through extensive study and practice, you may very well be on the right track.

The Music Umbrella

Next, you should know that a college music degree serves two purposes. First, the degree prepares you for a career by providing career-specific knowledge and skills that you will need as a music teacher, performer, composer, or whatever your chosen profession may be. The second, and perhaps more important, purpose of a college music degree is to help you become a better overall musician, regardless of your stated career goals.

First-year music majors commonly question why they need to take certain classes when they do not see how a particular course will help them in their individual career goals. To address this question, consider that there is an incredibly diverse range of careers that fall under the music label. While each career has its own unique job-related requirements and descriptors, all jobs are categorized as careers in music. All music careers, then, require the same fundamental level of musical knowledge and skill.

As a comparison, all medical doctors begin with a comparable premed degree program. As they progress in their training and professional experience, doctors find particular areas of medical study that interest them and begin to streamline their training into one specific area. Therefore, any cardiologist, gastroenterologist, or neurologist can perform the same, basic-level medical tasks, but can perform advanced tasks only in their respective areas of specialization.

Similarly, all professional musicians should be able to perform certain rudimentary musical tasks. While there is not a formalized, exhaustive inventory of basic musical skills, the list generally includes the ability to read music in multiple clefs, sing in tune, and play piano; knowledge of instruments; knowledge of music history; and an array of other abilities. These basic-level musical abilities serve as the musical foundation on which advanced, career-specific skills and abilities are built.

It may help you, then, to redefine the term *musician* as an umbrella that covers a broad range of knowledge and skills. In each career, you must possess certain job-specific knowledge and skills that will enable you to fulfill the professional duties of your chosen career. However, you must also possess a number of transferable skills and knowledge sets that are generalizable to all music careers. The college curriculum has been purposefully designed to prepare you for success as a musician, both in the broad sense and in the career-specific sense of the word.

SUCCESS AND CAREER COMPATIBILITY

The umbrella analogy, as it pertains to a redefinition of what it means to be a musician, gives credence to the assortment of skills and knowledge that you will no doubt encounter in your first years of formal music training. This new definition also indicates a very important aspect of becoming a professional musician that is commonly overlooked: talent is simply not enough to guarantee success in a music career. Nor will love of music alone be an accurate predictor for success as a musician.

Rather than success or talent, the key factor to consider when evaluating your potential as a professional musician is the concept of compatibility, or fit. Like pieces of a puzzle, your abilities, characteristics, quirks, mannerisms, and other traits all come together in a particular way to determine whether or not you may find success in a music career. However, you are only one half of the puzzle.

The other half of the puzzle is completed with pieces that identify job descriptions, professional responsibilities, and other traits of music careers. To complete the puzzle, you must evaluate the measure to which your traits, musical abilities, interests, and other attributes correlate to the professional responsibilities of the jobs in which you may be interested. To determine compatibility, you must first learn everything you can about yourself, and then compare your attributes to related music career traits to determine your potential fit, or suitability, in a music career.

Know Thyself

The first step of the career-advising process is to evaluate your attributes or personal traits that may determine your career compatibility. As is described in the introduction, there are four specific attributes that you should identify about yourself when considering a career in music:

1. What are your musical and nonmusical skills?
2. What are your musical and nonmusical interests?
3. What are your musical and nonmusical work values?
4. What are your personal characteristics?

Skills

To identify your skills, be honest with yourself about the musical and nonmusical tasks in which you naturally excel. Consider the subjects that you understand easily or the areas in which you seem to have a natural bent. It may also be helpful to consider the areas in which your peers look to you for help and your teachers look to you for leadership. These are strong indicators of your musical and nonmusical skills.

In chapter 1, it was noted that an honest self-evaluation can be painful at times. This can be especially true regarding our own perception of musical ability (skill). For example, you may have a strong desire to become a band, choir, or orchestra director. If, however, you do not have the ear to sing or perform in tune, you may not be able to get a school ensemble to perform in tune either. Similarly, if you want to become a performer but never win first chair in your school ensemble, you may need to consider another option. In either case, you must be fully, openly, and brutally aware of your musical and nonmusical skills.

Interests

The next and perhaps simplest questions to answer pertain to your interests. What do you like to do? How do you spend your spare time? What are you interested in, both from a musical and nonmusical perspective? As you consider your answers to these questions, also consider that interests are commonly linked to skills. A growing interest in a particular area may reveal a previously undiscovered or underdeveloped skill. As one is strengthened, the other may also become more fine-tuned.

Regarding interests, it may be common for students to believe that interests are only related to hobbies or other nonprofessional pursuits. In truth, your career satisfaction will be directly linked to your ability to pursue personal and musical interests in your job. Begin by making a list of things that are of interest to you, again, both musically and nonmusically speaking.

If you enjoy music and writing, for example, you may find enjoyment as a music critic. If you are interested in medicine or science, you may enjoy a career in music therapy. Each music career encompasses a unique grouping of musical and nonmusical interests that will help you determine your potential fit.

Work Values

Work values may be the most difficult concept of career advising to define. In simplest terms, work values may be identified by the ways in which you feel musically, personally, or professionally rewarded. Work values are revealed by the musical and nonmusical activities that bring you a sense of personal, professional, or musical satisfaction or gratification. Performers often say that they feel rewarded when they are able to bring life to a composition. Music teachers, however, express the same sensation when they help someone else feel successful as a musician.

There are a lot of other ways in which musicians feel rewarded through their jobs. However, as a young musician, you may not have experienced a broad enough array of musical experiences to determine the ways in which you feel rewarded. Therefore, you may experience difficulty in answering this question. If this is the case for you, remember: be patient, be industrious, and be inquisitive. Seek out opportunities that will expose you to a variety of music career options where you may begin to feel rewarded through your efforts.

Personal Characteristics

Lastly, you need to spend some time generating an extensive list of words that describe you, your personality, your disposition, your work ethic, your character, and everything about you. These words may describe your approach to life, music, schoolwork, or extracurricular activities. They may describe the way you keep or don't keep your room clean; the amount of time you study, practice, or listen to classical music; or anything else that describes you as a person or as a musician.

In this final category, it may be helpful for you to ask parents, teachers, and other adults whom you respect to help you generate a list. As you receive input, again, be humble and willing to receive brutally honest input. Sometimes, other people know you better than you know yourself. As you collect more information about yourself from a wide variety of resources, you will learn how others see you and will be able to use this feedback to determine the music career that may be the best fit for you.

Know Your Music Career Options

Once you have answered these four questions about yourself, the next step is to determine how your skills and other traits fit into one or more of the many available music careers. Each career requires a unique set of skills, feeds a particular set of interests, rewards its workers in a particular way, and requires certain dispositions that may be unnecessary in other careers. The next step in this process will help you determine the music career where you may be most suitable or compatible, and therefore experience more personal, professional, and musical satisfaction.

Begin by generating a list of music career opportunities that are of interest to you. Your first draft of this list may be as broad based as you want it to be, including careers that you may know only by name, were recommended in a career advising book, or were mentioned by a teacher or advisor. Bear in mind as you begin that simply listing a career does not commit you to anything. You can add to or delete from your list as often as you like.

Next, learn enough information about each career on your list to prioritize your options. You may find that the top choices may be the ones you had in mind all along simply because you knew more about them from the outset. The careers near the bottom may seem of little interest to you, but more research may reveal certain aspects of the career that may suit you very well. As you explore each option more thoroughly, you may begin to discover certain aspects about some of the jobs that do not coincide with your interests, skill set, or other traits. These options should obviously be removed or moved further down the priority list.

Finally, work with your teachers, parents, and advisors to determine how your skills and other attributes are related or dissimilar from the attributes for the top careers on your list. Once you have identified the career in which you are most interested, and that best suits your skills and other attributes, you are ready to begin the appropriate steps toward preparing for the chosen career.

IN YOUR FIRST YEARS

The process described previously has been designed to introduce a series of questions and answers that will help you make wise, well-informed career decisions. While there are many commonly accepted career-advising strategies, it must also be stated that there are no guarantees in predicting future success or compatibility.

Sometimes, after extensive research and experimentation, students are able to make clear, focused decisions that point to a very specific career path. If you are able to make these types of decisions, you will minimize the margin of error in selecting a career that may not be compatible with your skills and other interests.

Other times, students have only a general notion of what they do not want to do, rather than a clear idea of what they would like to do as a profession. Because their decision-making process lacks direction, they may easily miss the career choice with which they are most compatible. If you find yourself in this situation, take a few steps backward in the previously described career advising process and obtain more information that will enable you to make better decisions.

A healthy balance of open-mindedness and patience is also well advised for students who may still feel indecisive after a fair amount of music career research. In some cases, students may be a good fit in a music career path that may not have seemed initially interesting. Other times, there may be a wide variety of music careers to which students may not be exposed until later in their training. Therefore, you may simply need a little more time or may need to reevaluate options that you did not previously consider.

Although it is more desirable for students to have as much information as possible in the earlier phases of their decision-making processes, the reality is that some students are not exposed to certain music careers until after they have declared a major in an unrelated area. As a high school student, you may have been exposed only to a limited selection of music career options. In the first years of college, however, you will be required to take a variety of courses that may expose you to new areas of music in which you may be interested.

It is common in situations such as these for the new areas of interest to lead to music career choices that were previously unexplored. Consequently, it may be suitable in some circumstances to begin training for a career in music with only a general sense of career possibilities, rather than a specific career goal in mind.

Finally, it is important that you avoid making career decisions based on unrelated factors. As an example, a boyfriend or girlfriend may be considered an unrelated factor. Yes, some high school and college relationships lead to marriage, but this should not deter you from pursuing the most fitting degree or career for your skills and interests.

The anticipated amount of time it may take to complete a particular degree is also an unrelated factor. Although a degree with fewer required courses may seem more attractive at the outset, it may not always prepare you for a career that best suits you. In other words, do not select a degree plan that seems like the quickest or easiest way out of college. Instead, consider the degree as a financial and professional investment to the next thirty or more years of your life. Stay in college the extra semester or two that may be required in certain music degree programs to adequately prepare for the career that is most suited to your skills and interests.

Rather than relationships or the amount of time you may spend in college, the more pressing considerations to make are these:

- Does this career fit my strengths, interests, and abilities?
- Will I be personally and professionally satisfied in this career?
- Will this career allow me to have the kind of lifestyle I want to have?

The answers to these questions, in combination with a thorough awareness of music career options and your personal skills, interests, and other attributes, will enable you to make appropriate, informed career choices, and will prepare parents and teachers to help students make important career decisions.

Decisions, Results, and Pure, Dumb Luck

As you conduct research, make choices, and begin the steps toward a music career, you may observe that not every student experiences the same career-related struggles. You may wonder, then, if you have made the wrong choice or are going about your research incorrectly. Remember, however, that there are many types of music careers and an equally diverse group of people who want to become professional musicians. Also, there will be a number of different paths that lead to careers in music and different outcomes for different people.

In general, there are three types of people regarding career choices. First, there is a small group of individuals who know exactly what they want to do, seem to move effortlessly through the steps it takes to get there, and transition seamlessly from music student to professional musician. It is also common for these types of people to have been involved with music from a very young age, or to have grown up in a family of musicians in similar or identical careers.

Next, there are a number of laissez-faire people who do not have a clue as to what they want to do or become. In high school, they may participate in a variety of clubs, organizations, and extracurricular activities. When the time comes to decide on a college and potential degree, they choose to major in something that they like or in which they have had some experience. When they begin college, they may take a class that reveals previously untapped strengths or interests, and may choose for a while to major in the new area. After a few changes of major and related career goals, people in this category finally settle on a degree plan, graduate, and begin their careers, typically in a job that is not at all related to their original plans.

Finally, there are a number of people who know exactly what degree and career they want to pursue when they enter college. However, for this final category of students, the plans do not always work out as originally intended. In some cases, the change in plans is intentional. For other, the change is revealed or mandated.

Some students discover a new area of interest or giftedness and decide to change to a new major. In other cases, university faculty and administration are faced with the tough decision to inform students that they have not been admitted to a particular program. There are also situations where state or nationally mandated requirements for certain programs force students out of some music degrees. In these scenarios, students are faced with the realization that their original plan is not what they had bargained for or that they are not as suited for the particular career goal as they once thought they were.

Get Involved

A drawback of beginning college with only a vague idea of what you want to do is that it is easy to waste precious time and money trying to come to a final conclusion regarding your career goal. This pitfall also applies if you begin college without a thorough awareness of your skills, interests, and other abilities. And the deadly combination of these two snares only increases your likelihood of ignorance and indecisiveness in your music career decisions.

The most useful piece of advice to help you answer questions about yourself and about your potential suitability in a music career is *get involved*. You will not be able to answer some questions about yourself until and unless you experience musical and professional situations that will reveal your skills, interests, and other abilities. You will not know of your potential for success as a music teacher, for example, until you work with children in a student-teacher capacity. You will not know of your success in performance until you go through the process of winning and losing a variety of auditions.

In any music career field, the most effective answers to your career-advising questions will come through involvement. Therefore, as early as you can, find ways to get involved in the areas of music in which you may be interested as a career. Volunteer opportunities are available at many places of worship or at local community programs. Internships are available at many local music businesses. You may also find part-time employment teaching private lessons, in local music businesses, at summer camps, or in numerous other possibilities.

As you participate in these experiences, you will learn more about yourself and more about the career in which you may be interested. You may be introduced to certain skills you did not know you had or to music career opportunities you did not know were available. You will make personal and professional connections that will last a lifetime, and that may one day help you get a job.

You may also discover that you are not at all suited for the career in which you were initially interested. You may learn that there are aspects of a particular job that you dislike or do not coincide with your interests and abilities. If this happens, do not view the experience as a failure. Rather, view this as a learning experience that will guide you in a more appropriate direction and keep you from pursuing a career in which you will be miserable.

Career Assessments

Finally, there are a variety of personality assessments, skills identifiers, and other career-related tests that may help you identify your career suitability. School counselors, university admissions offices, and career advising centers commonly have updated copies of interest surveys and career inventories, if you choose to pursue this option. Many of these tests are linked to a database of careers that are prescribed upon completion of the test, based on your test results.

However, while these tests may provide extensive insight into your personality and skills, they may leave you feeling as though you are not a good fit for a music career, simply because a significant number of music career options are not represented in the test's database. A majority of these tests and career databases were not created by musicians and do not represent a full extent of music career options. Before you invest time and money into any of these services, inquire about the extent of music career options that may be prescribed upon completion of the test.

CONCLUSION

When you are unaware of key pieces of information about yourself and about the careers in which you may be interested, you are more likely to feel forced into career decisions for which you may not be suited. After a great amount of personal, musical, or professional frustration, you may begin to understand that you would have been better suited to a different career if you had known more information during the decision-making process.

However, a keen awareness of your skills, interests, and abilities, as well as a detailed knowledge of available music careers, will empower you to make better choices. Whether you have clearly defined career goals or only a general idea of what you would like to, your answers to the questions included in this chapter will guide you through the transition from student to music professional.

THREE

All About You

As you take your first steps toward a music career, you may be tempted to begin by exploring your career options. While this may seem like the right choice, a better place to begin is with you. An acute sense of self-knowledge will guide you in your decision-making process, as long as you begin with the right pieces of information about yourself.

As an example, you would never go to a Thai restaurant if you know you do not like Thai food. Nor would you apply for a job as an entomologist if you know you are afraid of insects. Relating this analogy to music career research, you must possess a keen awareness of your interests, skills, abilities, and other attributes before you begin investigating music career options. Only then will you be able to match your career goals with your skills and abilities.

As chapter 2 describes, there are four specific questions you should ask about yourself:

1. What are my musical and nonmusical skills?
2. What are my musical and nonmusical interests?
3. How do I feel personally, professionally, or musically rewarded?
4. What words describe my overall personality?

Your answers to these questions will help you align your attributes to the job descriptions, and the musical and professional requirements of each music career. Because there is such a diverse range of music career possibilities, there is an equally diverse array of skills, interests, and other attributes that are required for each music career.

While there are many career-specific attributes that will help you determine your potential fit in a music career, there are also generalizable or transferable attributes that are necessary for all professional musicians, regardless of specific career paths. This chapter will describe several transferable traits that are necessary for all music careers, and the extent to which each trait may impact your potential suitability for a career in music.

DESIRABLE SKILLS

As you evaluate your potential fit in a music career, first consider your musical and nonmusical skills and abilities. In each career, music or otherwise, there are specific tasks and job responsibilities that you will be expected to fulfill. If you are not well suited, or if your skills do not match the required tasks of your chosen career, you may quickly find yourself searching for other options.

As you read through the following information, make an honest self-assessment of whether or not you truly possess the required skills of your chosen career, and the extent to which the following information applies to you.

Performance Ability

First and foremost, you must be able to perform, either as a vocalist or on a primary instrument. Although performance ability may be an obvious requirement for some music careers, there are other careers where performance might seem less important. However, in any music career, your ability to perform and your experiences as a performer are crucial components for compatibility.

As you read this, you may be tempted to delete music from your list of career options, feeling that your lack of performance ability may keep you from getting a job. While performance ability is important, it is not the only required skill and should not be considered as the solitary criteria for success in a music career. More so, consider that all musicians perform, but the type of career you choose will determine both the amount of performance and the level of mastery as a performer that may be required of you.

Specifically, there were three particular words used by professional musicians who were interviewed for this book to describe the level of performance requirements for different types of music careers. Without fail, professional performers described the required level of performance ability for performing careers as a *mastery* of the instrument or voice. Music teachers used the word *proficient* to describe the necessary performance level. And a third group of musicians described the performance requirement as *competency* in a primary performance area.

Some may argue that the difference in the specific words used to express the need for performance ability is just an issue of semantics, meaning that the issue of performance is more important than the words selected to express the skill. Others, however, may suggest the particular words or phrases imply a hierarchy of performance ability in the various music careers.

Mastery

The term *mastery* implies that a performer has reached such a level of ability that he or she is considered an authority figure in his or her performance area. Naturally, performers need to have mastered their instruments or voices to obtain and maintain steady employment as career performers. Performers such as Yo-Yo Ma (cello), James Galway (flute), or Andrea Bocelli (voice) are key examples of those who have mastered their performance media.

These performers, and many others like them, help to clearly define what it means to have mastered a performance medium. First, performers need to have mastered the technique of their performance area. Technique implies intonation, articulation, diction, and all the other physical, technical, or mechanical aspects of their performance media.

Second, performers need to be masters of the related repertoire for their performance areas. Specifically, performers need to be masters of each musical style related to their performance media. In most cases, this implies a certain level of versatility or adaptability as most instruments and voice types are expected to perform in multiple genres and styles. In addition, performers must master the specific literature or musical selections that have become standards for their instrument or voice type. Just as clarinet players must master the Mozart "Clarinet Concerto," pianists must master Chopin's Nocturnes and tenors must master Verdi's "La Donna e Mobile."

Next, performers need to be masters of musical artistry. Artistry may also be defined as phrasing, flow, or general musicianship that enables a performer to move beyond the technique of merely singing or playing a piece of music, to truly making it worth the listener's time. Some may say that artistry is what sets performers apart from their musical counterparts in nonperformance careers. Any number of pianists, for example, can play Beethoven's *Moonlight Sonata*. An excellent performer, however, adds certain musical elements in such a way as to set his or her performance apart from any others.

Finally, true performers are masters of consistency. Most musicians have had moments of excellence, usually in the practice room and occasionally onstage. However, most musicians also struggle with inconsistency as performers. Those who perform incredibly well on Monday might not do as well on Tuesday, completely flop on Wednesday, and be fine again on Thursday. Musicians who consistently perform at an incredibly high level of excellence, however, set themselves apart as masters of their instruments or voices.

Proficiency

Music educators who were interviewed for this book used the word *proficient* to describe the level of performance needed in teaching careers. Proficiency suggests a level of performance that is well above average but may not yet be at the level of mastery described by performers. Also consider that the primary professional responsibility of performers is to perform, so it is natural to assume a different performance expectation of performers than of educators. In education, performance ability is one of many required attributes that contribute to the overall effectiveness of music teaching.

Also remember that while performers usually focus their efforts on one particular instrument, genre, or performance medium, educators must be proficient in many areas. Instrumental ensemble directors, for example, can usually play most if not every instrument in an ensemble at least well enough to teach a student how to play a particular part. Choral directors are also commonly equipped with a fundamental knowledge of instruments so they can conduct operas, oratorios, musicals, and the many other vocal/choral works that are accompanied by instrumental ensembles.

Finally, it is a common belief among music educators that you cannot be an effective music teacher if you are not, first, an effective musician. Notice, however, that the word *musician* has been used interchangeably with the word *performer*. Again, this may be nothing more than an issue of word choice. However, a noteworthy point that will be discussed at length in later sections of this chapter is that the terms *performer* and *musician* are not synonymous and should not be used interchangeably.

Competency

The third and final descriptor of required performance ability, *competency*, was used primarily by professionals in music business whose job descriptions mainly include administrative or technical work. Competence implies a certain level of skill as a performer, or perhaps that a musician has extensive experience as a vocal or instrumental performer. However, similar to music educators, music business professionals may be more skilled in other musical or nonmusical areas than performers. In essence, there must be a proportionate balance of performance ability and other skills that differ from one music career to another.

Potential for Mastery

As you ponder the type of music career you wish to pursue, it is vital for you to honestly evaluate your skill as a performer in your primary area. More so, you must evaluate your potential for mastery, proficiency, or competence. There are seldom few who may be considered masters of their instruments or voices when they are still in high school or college. Rather, most musicians demonstrate certain levels of potential in the earlier phases of their careers that is not fully revealed until later in life.

Also remember that even the most astute performer is also human. To master your instrument does not imply that you must become an invincible, omni-musical superhero performer. It simply means that your mistakes are few and far between, and that you deal well, both musically and professionally, with the mistakes that may happen during a performance.

To determine your potential for mastery, ask yourself two questions. First, are you really *that* good? You may be first chair or section leader in your school ensemble, but do you win competitions at the regional, state, or national levels? Many students expect that they will be good performers because they do well in their individual schools. However, when they begin college, they are suddenly surrounded by many other musicians who are as good as or better than they are, and they begin to realize that they may not be as good as they thought.

Also ask whether you acquire new skills easily. If not, do you enjoy the challenge of practicing as long as it takes to acquire those skills that do not come easily? Some performers seem immediately successful with new musical challenges. Others master certain tasks only after hours of diligent practice. As a performer, if you are not immediately successful in attaining new skills, it does not necessarily mean that you will not succeed. You must be willing, however, to devote the time it may take to become successful in these areas. If you are not immediately successful and you do not enjoy diligent practice, you may need to consider that your potential for mastery may not be at the level it takes to succeed in certain music careers.

Overall Musicianship

Earlier in this chapter, it was noted that the words *performer* and *musician* are commonly used as synonyms. Instead, consider that these are two different words to describe different but related characteristics of musicians. Specifically, performance is one of many means by which musicianship is revealed or conveyed to an audience.

Musicianship, on the other hand, may be better defined as an overall understanding or grasp of music that is revealed through excellence as a performer, music teacher, composer, or many other means. Sometimes musicianship is also defined as musicality, or a keen inner awareness of intonation, pitch, rhythm, and the other elements of music. This is also commonly identified as a good ear, musical aptitude, or more simply, talent.

There are innumerable musicians around the world who express their musicianship through nonperforming means. Composers, theorists, librarians, teachers, music historians, acousticians, and other professional musicians demonstrate their musicianship through means that are more appropriate to their career paths than performance, but are no less musical than their performing colleagues. Therefore, while it may not be necessary for you to be an incredibly strong performer, you must be an outstanding musician and be able to demonstrate that musicianship in one or more means.

Regardless of your particular career path, however, there are five universally required skills or abilities that you should possess as a musician. If you do not feel strong in these areas, remember that your first year or two of college will help you grow in these areas. First, you must be able to read music at an advanced level. Music literacy must also be coupled with at least a rudimentary knowledge of music theory. In addition, you must have a keenly developed musical ear, so that you can identify, analyze, and interpret multiple aspects of music. Next, you must be able to sing. This does not necessarily imply that you have to have an excellent voice, but that you can sing in tune. Finally, you must be able to play piano at a proficient level.

These skills and knowledge sets have been described as essential competencies for a music career. While some of these components can be acquired, other innate abilities are developed, and future training will refine your ability to use them effectively in your career. Similar to your potential for mastery-level performance, you must evaluate your potential for acquiring or developing each of these abilities. Whether you plan to teach, perform, compose, research, or conduct, these skills and abilities will be definitive aspects of your career as a professional musician.

In addition to the musical skills that have been discussed, there are many nonmusical skills that are essential for careers in music. In some cases, nonmusical skills may seem initially unrelated to music but have a significant impact on your ability to succeed in your chosen music career.

People Skills

First and foremost, you must be able to work well with people in a diverse range of professional settings. Even before you enter the career field, your ability to win your dream job may depend on the people skills necessary to build personal and professional connections that may lead to employment. This is not to suggest that the nicest people get the jobs, but more so that the cordial people, those with well-developed people skills, are the ones who are invited to the interviews and auditions.

Just as rudimentary people skills may lead to employment for some, a lack of people skills may limit or prohibit possible employment opportunities for others. Many musicians, particularly those in performance-based careers, have suggested that theirs is an incredibly small professional world and a person's reputation as a performer and as an individual can spread very quickly. It may therefore be difficult for musicians with questionable reputations to find work. Musicians also suggest that there are excessive numbers of professional struggles in music without the added aggravation of dealing with people who lack rudimentary people skills.

As an added analogy, consider this. There are usually between one hundred and two hundred candidates who audition for a vacant position in the major symphony orchestras and opera houses in the United States, and approximately half of these candidates could do the job well enough if they were hired. During the last phases of the audition process, however, each finalist usually rehearses with the other section members or perhaps performs a concert with the ensemble to test the candidate's overall compatibility with the section members. The attribute that makes the winning candidates stand out among the other applicants is their ability to relate to people on a personal and professional level.

In other music career fields, while there may not be as many job candidates, people skills are still an essential attribute for employment and career sustainability. If you own a music retail business, for example, you must be able to deal with rude or pushy customers, or you will lose your clientele. If you want to become a music teacher, you will eventually encounter irritable administrators, pushy parents, and the occasional quirky student. As a performer, you will most certainly come across at least one cantankerous conductor or perhaps a diva or two during your career.

As you read through this short list of examples, you may begin conjuring your own list of music careers where you feel people skills are not important. Performers, for example, spend most of their time in practice rooms, isolated from the world around them. Composers work primarily in their studios, behind computers and pianos. Some music librarians, historians, and other researchers spend their entire working day in the back rooms of music libraries.

People skills hardly seem necessary in careers where musicians spend most of their professional time secluded from social interaction. On the contrary, performers seclude themselves in practice rooms so that they can eventually take their music onto the stage to perform for live audiences. Similarly, composers utilize people skills to teach performers how to perform their work, teach audiences how to listen to it, and convince publishers to buy it. In each case where musicians seclude themselves for extended periods of time, the isolation is short lived when compared to the amount of time that musicians spend dealing with people. Therefore, people skills are essential for obtaining and maintaining employment in music.

Business Skills

A second nonmusical skill that is desirable for professional musicians is business skill. While people skills may imply a clearly defined set of attributes, business skills encompass a broader range of aptitudes. These abilities include marketing, production, administration, contract negotiation, accounting, entrepreneurialism, and for a host of other possibilities.

If you want to work in the music industry, for example, you may pursue a career as an agent, promoting your clients' music to publishing companies, producers, and record labels, and securing concert dates and locations. Or, you may work as a producer, organizing concerts, generating budgets, and hiring musicians for concert performances, among other duties. In each case, you will need to rely on a variety of business skills to perform your daily tasks.

One of the more common business skills that is essential for music careers is entrepreneurialism. As it pertains to musicians, entrepreneurialism describes a go-for-it mentality of people who possess drive, initiative, and innovation, particularly among musicians who forge their own careers using innovative marketing strategies to promote themselves in their career fields.

There are many musicians, especially in performance-related career fields, who piece together a number of part-time, freelance opportunities. This is especially true for younger musicians who are just beginning to work their way into the career field. In essence, these musicians market themselves as musicians by promoting their recordings, publicizing their upcoming performances, and making their names known in their field. If this describes your career goals, you must possess a keen sense of entrepreneurialism that will enable you to implement the most effective tactics that will generate a market for your music and for yourself as a musician.

Another business skill that is essential in many music career fields is accounting. On a large scale, every music corporation hires musicians who understand both the musical and the financial aspects of the company. If you are interested in music and are also gifted with numbers, you may be an accountant for a music publishing company, performance organization, record label, concert hall, instrument manufacturer, or music retail store.

On a smaller scale, there are aspects of every musician's job wherein financial skills are essential. Many performing musicians piece together a number of part-time jobs and rely on financial skills to compile a number of smaller incomes and report them accurately on income tax documents. These musicians may also experience extended periods of unemployment and depend on accounting to budget their income to last during long periods of unemployment.

Music educators also utilize accounting skills to maintain departmental budgets, keep accurate records of fundraising dividends, organize finances for field trips and ensemble tours, and for a host of other duties. Musicians who teach private lessons commonly have up to fifty or more students each week and must accurately track an irregularly occurring income based on attendance, lesson length, holidays, and other factors that determine how much a student pays each month.

As a final example, many musical theater performers work in seasonal theme parks to finance a temporary move to New York to audition for Broadway musicals or other productions. If, at the end of an audition season, a musician has not won an audition, he or she may return to a temporary role in theme park performances to prepare for the next year's round of auditions. In these scenarios, musicians commonly have little to no income during audition seasons and rely on savings generated from seasonal employment.

These scenarios reveal the significance of business skills for professional musicians, particularly those in music business, performance careers, or other venues where musicians may be self-employed. Therefore, as you consider your fit in a music career, think about your abilities in these areas. There are courses in high school and college that you can take to help you in areas where you may feel deficient. Specifically focus on personal finance, marketing, promotion, public relations, and business administration. These skills will be essential components of your potential for compatibility and success in a music career.

INTERESTS

Just as your skills will determine your potential for success in a music career, your interests should also play an essential role in the decision-making process. It is also common for your skills to be directly linked to your interests, or for your interests to reveal skills that may develop as you pursue an interest. As you read through the following information, consider your musical and nonmusical interests, and how they might be developed into professional pursuits.

You may also need to review your inventory of musical and nonmusical skills to look for connections between your skills and interests. When you make this comparison, remember two things. First, as has been stated, there may be a host of musical opportunities to which you have not yet been exposed. Second, remember that interests develop and change over time, especially as you are exposed to new elements. Therefore, keep an open mind about your current interests, information that generates new areas of interest, and how it all relates to your potential for compatibility in a music career.

Exposure through High School Performing Ensembles

Each musician interviewed for this book was asked about the musical and nonmusical interests that typically lead students to pursue a career in music. The most common answer to this question was that students' interest in music is typically generated through participating in high school performing ensembles. Although this response may not be clearly categorized as an interest, it is important to note that the experiences students gain in high school often lead to professional pursuits.

Initially, you may have been interested in pursuing a career in music because of your participation in high school ensembles. Usually, performance in high school ensembles develops into a natural desire to continue in music performance as a professional pursuit. You may also feel led to pursue a career in music education because of your experiences in school music programs and the impact your ensemble directors had on you as a student musician.

When you arrive on a university campus, however, you will be exposed to other programs offered by your university music department and may be able to utilize previously untapped aspects of your musicianship. This exposure to new opportunities may reveal previously undiscovered abilities and interests that may directly impact your career decisions. Through exposure to new opportunities, you may discover that your abilities lie in composition, theory, music therapy, or some other music career field of which you were unaware when you made your initial career decision.

Therefore, as you consider your interests, also remember that there are areas of music that you may not yet know exist. Yes, you can read about music career opportunities in a number of different books on the subject, but you will be able to measure your level of interest only by becoming involved in a wide array of experiences. Also, keep an open mind about career options as you experiment with new opportunities. Your open-mindedness may lead you to new areas of study and generate interests that that may redirect your career goals.

Fame and Fortune

An additionally common answer to the question of interests that lead students to pursue a career in music was fame and fortune. However, all musicians who provided this answer did so disdainfully and clarified that their answer should be interpreted as humor rather than sincerity. Musicians further indicated that fame and fortune may be one of the most common misconceptions of music careers, and may mistakenly lead people to pursue careers in music.

Whereas some musicians may achieve a certain status or financial stability, there is little consideration for fame and fortune among professional musicians. While some may desire fame or glory, this expectation is rarely fulfilled in music careers. Musicians who pursue careers in music for reasons other than purely musical satisfaction are the most likely candidates for professional failure and burnout. Therefore, musicians who enter music careers seeking fame and fortune may be deeply disappointed.

As you think about your own possible desire for fame and fortune, consider two points. First, you may need to define, or redefine, the difference between *fame* and a *career*. While some performers may achieve a certain level of fame, notoriety may quickly dissolve and the performer's career may end. There are countless examples of famous musicians, mainly performers, who quickly rose to stardom, enjoyed five to ten years in the spotlight, and then disappeared as quickly as they came.

However, behind every short-term famous musician, there is a host of average Joes who enjoy thirty or more years of professional satisfaction in their music careers. The sound engineer, for example, will still be able to operate the sound board for the next upcoming star when today's diva is no longer popular. Therefore, there may be greater career stability and permanence in careers that are not contingent on fame.

Second, most musicians are not motivated by the desire for fame, but more so by an intrinsic desire to be involved with music and the gratification of financially supporting themselves through that desire. Just as fame is fleeting, so, too, is the income that comes from a short-term career in the spotlight.

Therefore, redefine your paradigm of success in a music career. Success does not depend on fame, except for a select few. Rather, redefine success as the ability to stay professionally involved with music for a career that spans a lifetime. Also, redefine success as the ability to financially support yourself doing what you love.

WORK VALUES

Work values are revealed by the ways in which you feel personally, professionally, or musically rewarded in your work as a musician. Work values are strongly linked to the satisfaction you feel when you perform, teach, compose, conduct, or participate with music through other means. As you read this section, think about the musical and nonmusical activities that bring you the most enjoyment and generate a strong sense of satisfaction or gratification.

Helping Others

Almost all the musicians who were interviewed for this book stated that they felt the most personal and musical satisfaction from helping other people through their music. Church music leaders, teachers, music business professionals, music therapists, and many others all stated that they felt rewarded by helping other professional and avocational musicians become successful in their musical endeavors. A key differentiation was that some felt rewarded by working with professional musicians, and others by working with nonmusicians.

There are many music careers in which professional musicians work directly with nonmusicians on a daily basis. Music teachers, music therapists, and religious music leaders work mainly with nonmusicians either to help them become successful at musical tasks or at using music as a tool for nonmusical goals. These musicians commonly feel rewarded by helping nonmusicians understand music and becoming at least moderately successful in musical endeavors.

In other music careers, however, professional musicians work mainly with other musicians in a variety of settings. University music faculty members work primarily with student musicians to prepare them for careers as musicians. Composers and conductors help performers understand music better and elevate the performer's ability to succeed. Music business professionals commonly work behind the scenes to promote the career of performing musicians. In these situations, musicians feel rewarded through the success of the other musicians with whom they work.

Consequently, you need to consider whether you are pursuing a music career for your own gratification or for the impact that your professional endeavors may have on other people. Even the famous or well-known musicians who were interviewed for this book stated that they did not feel a sense of gratification from wealth or fame. However, they expressed satisfaction in knowing that their efforts benefited other people. Your desire to serve yourself or to serve other people through your music will be a key factor in determining your potential for suitability in a music career.

PERSONAL CHARACTERISTICS

There are countless ways in which you might describe yourself or in which other people might describe you. These descriptors of your personality are as important as skills, interests, and work values in evaluating your potential for success as a professional musician. While different types of people may be better suited for different types of music careers, there is one common trait, or personal characteristic, that is desirable in all music careers: tenacity.

Tenacity

A point that has already been discussed but bears repeating here is that there are thousands of musicians attempting to enter the career field, and all are competing for a comparatively small number of available jobs. This is especially true for any music career related to performance. You must therefore possess the tenacity and determination to endure the career struggles, fierce competition, the ability to work without recognition for extended periods of time, and other difficulties related to music careers.

There are also rigorous aspects of nonperforming music careers that will test your determination. Some music career preparation programs— namely, music education and music therapy, require you to pass licensure or certification exams that are mandated by state teacher organizations or nationally based professional associations. Other programs that may not require licensure exams do set high musical and academic standards wherein your determination, or tenacity, will be a crucial element of your success.

Tenacity may imply your determination or stick-to-itiveness, particularly in the earlier stages of your career. Tenacity may also imply your ability to work without recognition for an extended period of time. As an example, there are a number of musical masterpieces that were ignored when they were composed and did not achieve any significant popularity until well after the composer's death. Similarly, teachers may never see the rewards of their labor except in rare instances when students or parents demonstrate gratitude. Consequently, tenacity may be linked to intrinsic motivation, or the ability to work without recognition, in addition to the more commonly accepted associations to dedication and work ethic.

Returning to the overall concept of tenacity, there are three questions to ask of yourself to honestly assess your level of persistence: Do you possess the dogged determination it will take to manage the fiercely competitive work environment of performance careers? Or, will you be better suited in a music career that is less contingent on competition? Even still, might you experience greater success and professional satisfaction in a nonmusical career, and maintain involvement in music as hobby? Your answers to these questions reveal your level of tenacity as a key element for determining your potential for success in a music career.

CONCLUSION

Before you leave this chapter, return to your mental or written list of attributes that describe you, both as a musician and as a person. Refine your inventory of your musical and nonmusical skills and interests. Redefine the aspects of music or your other work that generate a sense of satisfaction for you. Revise the words that describe your personality. Fully consider every word on each list as it pertains to the information discussed in this chapter. This process will guide your decision as you move on to the chapters that provide career-specific information pertaining to skills, interests, work values, and personal characteristics.

FOUR

Music Career Trends

The initial step of career advising is to identify your skills, interests, and other traits that will help you identify your potential fit in a music career. The second step is to acquire as much information about the careers in which you are interested to see how well your traits correlate with job functions, professional responsibilities, and other descriptors of each potential career path.

Just as certain skills, interests, and other abilities are desirable in all music careers, there are characteristics of music careers that describe professions in multiple music career paths. This chapter describes four characteristics that are generalizable to most, if not all, music careers. Because the purpose of this chapter is to provide only generalized information, you may be left with further questions about specific music career options. Career-specific information is available in one or more of the chapters in part 2 of this book.

NONMUSICAL JOBS IN MUSIC CAREER FIELDS

The first commonality is that there may be a number of careers for non-musicians that exist within music career fields. A musical theater, for example, employs numerous musicians, but also relies on the skills of costume designers, set builders, lighting designers, and a host of additional people who may be considered nonmusical. Likewise, many music business careers are available to people with training and experience in intellectual property rights, accounting, management, and other administrative areas.

There are two ways of thinking about careers of this nature. First, these types of careers may be excellent options for people who are interested in music, but whose skills lie in other areas. In this light, as you evaluate your own skills and abilities, take particular stock in your overall level of musicianship. Also consider your nonmusical skills and interests as they apply to this scenario. While you may be innately interested in music and desire to associate yourself with musicians, you may be more suited for one or more of these types of careers where your nonmusical skills and abilities will be a greater professional asset than your musicianship.

In contrast, there is a different way of thinking about nonmusical careers in music career fields. Nonmusical careers are a necessary component of their related music career fields. The person driving the equipment truck or setting the stage, for example, may be an aspiring performer who took a technical job to learn as much about the business as possible. Similarly, the technical and design careers in musical theater may not require musical skill, but they are essential to the performance and may therefore be categorized among other music careers in the field.

If technical and design careers are accurately categorized as nonmusic careers, they may be suitable options for students with an interest in music, but who may be more skilled in these other areas than in music. If this describes your situation, you may need to consider whether a music degree is the best option for you, or if you would benefit more from a nonmusical degree program, with a possible minor in music.

Nonmusical careers in music career fields may also be suitable options for musicians aspiring to enter a particular music career path and choose an entry-level position or nonmusical career to get a foot in the door. If you aspire to perform on Broadway, in a large symphony orchestra or opera company, or in professional recording studios, consider your additional nonmusical skills and the possibility of putting these skills to use as you work your way into a performing career.

CROSS-CATEGORIZATION OF MUSIC CAREERS

Next, it is common to find many music careers categorized in a number of different music career classifications. To simplify this statement, certain music career labels mean different things to musicians in different career fields. While this seems like a miniscule issue, it may generate confusion as you attempt to determine the most appropriate college degree to pursue based on your potential music career goals. This also impacts the variety of skills you may need to succeed in a career field where there is so much crossover from one job to another.

As a specific example of a career that may be categorized in multiple fields, composing music may be grouped in as many as three classifications depending on the genre of the composition. A career in composition for wind ensembles, orchestras, choirs, or other standard ensembles would be most closely associated with a composition degree. Many music business degrees also offer courses in composition but primarily address digital music for video game soundtracks and songwriting for radio music. Composition may also apply to multiple venues of jazz music that commonly carry over into rock genres.

Similarly, performing may be a career opportunity in as many as three music career fields. Naturally, performance careers are available in symphony orchestras, chamber music, churches, opera companies, and pit orchestras for musical theater, or ballet companies. To a musician in the music industry, performance implies recording studios and live performance of various popular music genres. Performance is also applicable to the field of jazz studies through recording studios, live performance, clubs, and churches. Musical theater performance opportunities are available on cruise ships and in theme parks, live theaters, and touring companies.

Related to this issue is the reality that many professional musicians hold more than one job, usually in more than one music career category. Most music theorists, for example, are also active composers or performers. Most composers also conduct, perform in local ensembles or as soloists, or teach theory and composition courses in high schools or colleges. Lastly, it is common to find musicians in any career field who also hold part-time performance careers in various pickup ensembles (ensembles that assemble only on an as-needed basis).

As you consider how your own career goals fit into these scenarios, consider two main implications. First, be very purposeful in your career decisions and in choosing the most appropriate major for your career goals. This will also impact the type of university that you choose as different music departments emphasize different aspects of each degree. For example, a music business degree from a college in Los Angeles may focus more on studio work. The same degree from a college in New York City, however, may focus more on live performance.

Next, remember that there is a wide array of music career opportunities within each career path and that many musicians work in more than one area. You will be well served by an open-minded approach to music study and by exposing yourself to multiple musical experiences in high school and college. Diverse opportunities will improve your versatility as a musician and enable you to obtain employment more easily than your colleagues who are able to function only in a narrow range of venues.

MUSIC CAREERS IN TRANSITION

The third issue related to music career categorization is that many music career fields are consistently in states of transition. Technology, economy, musical trends, and many other factors have significant impacts on music careers that make it difficult at times to predict music career options. In some cases, innovations are cyclical, meaning that particular innovations may reoccur in predictable patterns, making it easier for musicians to predict upcoming changes. Other innovations are developmental, occurring only once, but leaving an impact that affects music careers for multiple generations.

Performance

Professional symphonies, opera houses, and other performance organizations are currently experiencing significant changes as a result of recent economic decline. Financial concerns commonly lead to a subsequent downsizing of the performance, condensed performance calendars, or smaller ensemble membership. Also, as a direct result of the current recession, there are fewer professional ensembles for which performers may audition than were available to previous generations. New generations of performing musicians may experience more success in solo careers or chamber music than through auditioning for major symphonies or opera companies.

Sacred Music

Current trends and musical tastes also change over time and may result in the creation, evolution, or elimination of some music careers. Regarding sacred music careers, for example, there is a current shift in many churches away from traditional worship formats to a more contemporary style of church music. A church music director in a traditional format may have needed conducting skills, the ability to lead a choir, skill at the piano or organ, and knowledge of hymnology.

In the contemporary format, however, a music director may need guitar skills and knowledge of contemporary music styles rather than, or in addition to, conducting and knowledge of hymnology. An additional change in sacred music is that at one point, most congregations sought to hire seminary-trained church musicians to lead worship. In the current trend, however, congregations may seek to hire nondegreed musicians with little formal musical training and a musical style that relates more to nonmusical congregants.

Pedagogy

Changes are also under way in the field of music pedagogy. As a brief aside, *pedagogy* commonly refers to musicians who teach private lessons out of their homes or in a studio housed in a local music retail store, community center, or place of worship. While there may be similarities between music education and music pedagogy, there are stark differences in the job descriptions and in the required training for each program.

Currently, many public schools have recently begun to acquire digital keyboard labs or implement string programs at the elementary and secondary levels. This trend may result in the ability for musicians trained in pedagogy to begin working in public school music classrooms. This trend may also result in the need for musicians seeking careers in pedagogy to take additional courses to pass state teacher certification or licensure exams and become state-certified music teachers. This may also necessitate further training in classroom management for teachers whose previous experiences may have centered chiefly on private instruction.

Musical Theatre

Innovations are also under way in musical theater. Specifically, the performance expectations in musical theater have vastly expanded in recent years to include particular skills that were not required of prior generations of performers. A recent production of *Sweeney Todd*, for example, required a singer to play an instrument onstage. *Spiderman* on Broadway requires the lead performer to execute staged combat scenes while suspended by cables from the rafters.

These innovations have redefined the *triple threat* stereotype of musical theater performers. In prior generations, musical theater performers were considered a triple threat if they could sing, act, and dance. Current innovations, however, may add instrumental performance, stage combat, or any number of skills to the list of requirements. As a result, musical theater professionals may need to seek additional training that will prepare them for an increasingly diverse range of performance expectations.

Music Business/Industry

Many of the recent changes in the music industry have been a direct impact of the changes in technology that occur at a blinding pace. Specifically, digital audio has had a significant impact on the number and types of jobs available in the music industry. Primarily, Internet-based marketing techniques have made it possible for musicians to promote their own music without relying on record companies or music publishers. OK Go and Pomplamoose are two of many examples of recording artists who have had greater success through the Internet than through traditional means.

Furthermore, many jobs that previously existed in CD production and sales may no longer be needed as a result of digital media. In prior generations, the release of a CD required label designers, people to copy CDs from the master recording to the mass-produced CDs, people to package the final product, sales people to market the CD to local stores, and a host of additional employees. A digital sound file that is immediately posted on a band's website, however, does not rely on such a large group of people to produce the recording. While this significantly reduces the cost of recorded music, it also drastically reduces the number of jobs that are available in the music industry.

Technology has also impacted the type of person who may become a performer of popular music. Pitch correction software and other technological applications are able to alter a performer's voice to disguise poor musicianship, make corrections to notes that are performed off pitch, and make other adjustments to a performer's voice or instrument. This technology has made it much easier for lesser-talented musicians to become performers of popular music.

Music Education

Lastly, there are a number of significant changes in music education. Instructional technology that has impacted classroom teaching methods across the country is increasingly becoming commonplace in general music classrooms and rehearsal halls. Music teachers who previously relied on CD players, tuners, and metronomes as their only means of technology are now expected to use SMART Boards, iClickers, virtual teaching methods, and many of the other applications previously available only to classroom teachers. There are also a multitude of cell phone applications (apps) devoted to music educators.

Music education has also been impacted by the recent popularization of alternative certification programs. Alternative certification has made it possible for nondegreed and noncertified musicians to become music educators in school districts that employ alternatively certified educators. As a result, certified music educators may feel additional competition for employment from nonlicensed teachers in a career field that was previously devoted solely to certified professionals.

Lastly, the emphasis on assessment, or standardized testing, that has been commonplace in the general classroom for generations is gradually working its way into the music curriculum. Seasoned music educators who have taught for years without the pressures of formalized assessment must modify their teaching methods to include new assessment expectations. University music teacher programs are also adapting their curricula to ensure that the next generation of music educators is prepared for new assessment requirements in music education.

Conclusion

Ideally, university music programs are on the cutting edge of music career innovations as they occur. More so, university music faculty members are the leaders of effective innovations, and the resistance of innovations that may have negative consequences. While your college experiences should prepare you to deal with the changes related to your particular career field, you must also do what you can to stay abreast of current advances that may impact you. A keen awareness of current events will improve your ability to predict reoccurring trends with a higher degree of accuracy, and thereby contend with the changing expectations of your music career field.

MUSIC DEGREE REQUIREMENTS

Lastly, professional musicians who were interviewed for this book were asked about the availability of careers in their fields to musicians who do not possess a college degree. In all music career fields except music therapy, professional musicians stated that most careers may be available to nondegreed musicians in their respective areas of specialization.

Even though a degree in music may not be required for many music careers, most professional musicians still feel compelled to convince music students of the importance of obtaining a music degree. While there may be musicians who successfully enter their chosen music careers without the related degree, there are significant advantages of obtaining a degree in music.

Specifically, the process of obtaining a degree will provide you with a structured, systematic opportunity to learn the skills and knowledge bases that will be required in your related career. It will also provide opportunities for you to learn these skills and concepts from professionals with extensive experience and training in the career fields.

Most students who choose to drop out of college to pursue music careers find themselves working in coffee shops, fast-food restaurants, or retail stores for financial support while auditioning for performing opportunities, applying for entry-level internships in the music industry, and building social and professional networks in their related career fields. This practice may directly relate to the number of out-of-work musicians trying to break into their respective music career fields, and the even greater number of would-be musicians who settled for nonmusical careers.

Those who choose to pursue a music career by first obtaining the related degree, however, will reap multiple benefits of four or more years of formal music study. A university music degree program prepares you for greater levels of success in your chosen career path with a systematic and rigorous program of study. It also connects you to professional musicians across the country who may one day enable you to find employment as a musician. Finally, a degree in music may quicken the pace with which you may ascend the career ladder in your chosen field.

If you are weighing your options regarding a degree in music, think about these options. Because a number of music careers do not require a degree in music, it may be advisable to take advantage of all music opportunities that come your way, even if an opportunity may result in a temporary withdrawal from a college music program. If the opportunity is temporary, you may return to college to complete the degree once the job is complete. Conversely, jobs will still be available after you have completed a college degree. It may also be advisable to avoid engaging in opportunities that may deter you from completing your degree before you are ready to enter the workforce.

CONCLUSION AND TRANSITION

This chapter describes four characteristics that describe music careers in a variety of career fields. To review, nonmusical jobs in music career fields may be viewed as entry-level positions for aspiring musicians or as career options for people with interests in music but skills in other areas. Next, there are various titles for some music careers, and these careers commonly exist in multiple career fields. Third, economic circumstances, musical trends, technology, and other elements directly impact the number of available music careers and the functions of these careers. Finally, while most music careers are available to nondegreed musicians, there are significant advantages of completing a music degree before pursuing a music career.

This chapter may have also generated more questions than answers related to job titles, job functions, or other issues about music career opportunities. The following chapters will elaborate on this information and provide additional characteristics of each music career field. These chapters will also describe the career-specific skills, interests, and other attributes that will help you determine your potential compatibility.

It is not the purpose of this book, however, to provide extensive, detailed descriptions of each and every music career. This book's primary purpose is to provide a general overview of each music career field, with a chief focus on the personal attributes of professional and aspiring musicians so that you can determine your potential fit in a music career. The annotated bibliography located in the appendix of this book describes additional music career resources that are specific to a particular music career field. These resources provide more detailed analyses of the music careers in their respective fields.

FIVE

Bachelor of Music in Performance

Careers in performance are perhaps the most visible and commonly known music career paths, with the possible exception of music education. Performance can also be one of the most misunderstood and challenging music career fields.

As of this writing, there are more universities that offer performance degrees than any other undergraduate music degree. This may erroneously indicate that there is an equitable number of careers available in performance. The reality is that there are far fewer jobs available in performance than there are people to fill those jobs.

In any given year, there are approximately 6,000 college students graduating with bachelor's degrees in performance, and only 400 full-time vacancies in the major performing ensembles across the country. To strengthen this argument, the number of people applying for those 400 jobs may be multiplied fivefold or more when considering the thousands of previous years' graduates who have not yet found employment, and the inestimable numbers of people who may pursue music careers without formal training.

While the situation may seem bleak, there are a number of alternatives that have become viable options for performing musicians. First, rather than auditioning for major symphonies or opera companies, many musicians have fulfilled their dreams by supplementing performance endeavors with nonmusical jobs while touring in a variety of freelance ensembles. Other performing musicians have forged their own careers by piecing together a number of part-time performing jobs or marketing themselves as solo or chamber performers, and maintaining careers as recitalists or soloists.

Whether you pursue a traditional performing career through auditions into the major ensembles or create a career for yourself through nontraditional means, performance can be a very rewarding career field. You will succeed only as much as you are willing to work and will be challenged to work harder than you thought possible.

CAREER ENTRY

In many careers, you will not be considered for a job until and unless you have completed a college degree in the related area. In music performance, however, the key ingredient for career entry is mastery of your voice or instrument. Professional performers usually agree that a college degree is less important unless you plan on teaching at the college level. Specifically, one performing musician who was interviewed for this book stated, "The degree is no guarantee of one's ability to perform." A second performer stated, "No one is going to ask if you have a degree or not."

In performance-related careers, obtaining a degree is more about networking and career preparation provided through the process of obtaining the degree. Performers who suggested that a degree is not required also suggested that it is highly recommended for aspiring performers to pursue an undergraduate degree. Through your course work, you will study from professionals in the field, learn the repertoire for your voice or instrument, and generate a professional network of other musicians that may lead to auditions and future employment. Without this network, you may easily find yourself lost in the crowd or feel as though you are one of thousands of other musicians all auditioning for the same job.

THE JOBS

As stated, performance careers are among the more visible, yet misunderstood, careers in music. Specifically, many nonmusicians may underestimate the variety of professional venues for performing musicians. Nonmusicians may also fail to recognize the incredible diversity of performance genres available to different voice types or instrumental specialization.

Musicians may perform in opera companies, symphony orchestras, musical theaters, cruise ships, theme parks, pit orchestras for ballet companies, touring shows, or professional chamber music ensembles. They may also obtain employment performing in churches or recording studios. There are also extensive opportunities performing in military ensembles.

Performers may also teach either at the college level or in a private studio setting. There are also performers who piece together a full-time income through entering performing competitions that offer a monetary prize. Other performers work with instrument manufacturers in the research and development of new instruments. Finally, many performers work their way into administrative jobs within the performing organizations or companies where they have previously performed.

MOST PROMISING LOCATIONS

The most promising locations for performers are usually in larger metropolitan areas where the opportunities are more abundant. In rural areas, performers commonly play or sing in a number of part-time (or pickup) orchestras, community bands, or vocal ensembles. It is also more common for performers in rural areas to have nonmusical jobs during the day and perform on evenings and weekends.

An additional specification regarding the most promising locations for performers is based primarily on your instrument or voice type, and your professional goals. If you wish to perform in a live setting of some kind, you may need to move to any large city with a number of performance halls and ensembles. If you wish to perform popular music, you may need to move to Los Angeles, Nashville, or New York, where recording companies and studios are more abundant. The major consideration you must make is the type of job(s) you want to have and the type of city in which you wish to live.

WHAT DOES IT TAKE TO BE A GOOD FIT IN PERFORMANCE?

Musical Skills

When performers were asked what musical skills were needed for compatibility in their chosen careers, many felt that the answer should be obvious: you must first be an incredible performer. Many went so far as to say that you must have mastered your instrument or voice. In addition, as so many performers are employed in a variety of professional ensembles, you must be a very versatile performer in that you must be able to perform music in a variety of styles and genres if you wish to maintain steady employment.

As you begin your training toward a performance career, your instructors will not expect you to have mastered your instrument or voice, but they will evaluate your potential for mastery. In addition, they will evaluate your overall musicianship and your willingness to work in the areas in which you need improvement. This should serve as a motivation to all potential performers to practice and at least demonstrate potential for mastery in the early phases of your career.

Performers also suggested that you need to have a very strong overall sense of musicianship, must have ear-training skills, and must be able to sight-read, again in a variety of musical styles. You need to be musically creative, able to think outside of the box, and apply a variety of musical elements to your performances until you find the combination of sounds that suit the conductor or section leader.

You need to be able to prepare your part well, usually without much guidance from a teacher or section leader. Performers frequently get a list of performance selections well in advance and are expected to listen to a variety of recordings, identify difficult phrases or melodies, and come to the first rehearsal with their parts well polished. In other instances, performers may receive their music only a day in advance or at the first rehearsal and must work quickly to prepare their part before the next day's rehearsal.

Finally, you must be able to maintain your instrument or voice throughout the duration of your career. There are many techniques that enable performers to sing higher or play louder, for example, than the competition, but that cause long-term damage to the performer. Brass players, for instance, commonly use excessive pressure on their embouchures to play in the upper register. Vocalists attempting to emulate the sounds of operatic or popular singers may sing well out of their registers and cause extensive long-term damage to their vocal chords. Tendencies such as these may provide short-term results but will significantly diminish the sustainability of a performer's career.

Nonmusical Skills

Because there is such an unduly crowded job market in performance, people skills are the most essential nonmusical skill for building social networks that will eventually lead to steady employment. It is also helpful if you have a business background as you will most likely spend a great deal of time marketing yourself as a performer, juggling a number of part-time schedules and incomes, and in many cases, may also perform some sort of business function in the ensembles in which you perform. Performers also need to have good teaching skills, and time-management skills, and be able to work well on a team.

Musical Interests

Because your professional time will most likely be consumed by your instrument/voice, preparing for auditions and rehearsals, and teaching others about your instrument/voice, you need to have a general love of music, of your instrument or voice, and of the genres in which you will most commonly perform. You should also have an interest in teaching as performers commonly spend a majority of their time teaching either in a private or classroom setting. Finally, performers commonly express a desire to emulate a famous performer in their field. Therefore, it is helpful if you are interested in listening to and analyzing the performances of well-known performers in your particular area of interest.

Nonmusical Interests

When performers were asked about the nonmusical interests that led them to pursue a career in performance, many stated, "It's all about the music." This is not to indicate that performing musicians lead one-sided lives, but more that their entire professional identity is bound to their sole interest in performing. Therefore, as a performer, you should have a strong desire to rehearse and perform, and find yourself generally consumed by music.

Performers also commonly feel drawn or called to the stage. Rather than self-fulfilling goals, it is more common for performers to suggest that their desire to be onstage is not driven by pride, but more so by a desire to help others through their music. Therefore, you should have a general desire to connect with people and to find ways to benefit other people through performing.

Musical Work Values (How You Feel Musically Rewarded)

Performing musicians feel rewarded when they are able to produce beautiful music and communicate with an audience through their performance. They love playing the great music by great composers in their fields and performing at a very high level with other great performers. Many of them also feel rewarded by the process of practicing a difficult piece and seeing it develop from the first read-through to the first performance.

Therefore, a key indicator of your potential for compatibility as a performer is the sense of accomplishment you may feel when you are able to connect to an audience and to other performers onstage. You may also feel driven to become a better performer through a desire to have a deeper connection to your audience. This drive may also generate a deeper sense of personal satisfaction that comes from seeing the direct result of diligent practice.

Nonmusical Work Values (How You Feel Personally or Professionally Rewarded)

Many performers who were interviewed for this book stated that they had a difficult time separating musically rewarding from personally or professionally rewarding. For them, the two were inseparable. You, too, may not be able to differentiate the sense of accomplishment that comes from performance as a musical accomplishment or a personal accomplishment.

Generally, performers feel rewarded by the ability to inspire other people through their music. This may mean inspiring others to become better performers, better people, or perhaps inspiring a love of music in a person who would otherwise have no musical interests. Finally, performers enjoy being able to travel, teach, and have the ability to make a living doing what they love.

Personal Characteristics

Performers suggest that theirs is the most difficult of all music career fields in which to find and maintain steady employment. Therefore, the most commonly cited personal characteristics in this field are work ethic, discipline, and tenacity. Performers suggest that you must be willing to work very diligently for long periods of time without reward. This is an especially essential skill given the saturated job market that was already discussed. Also, for younger performers, tenacity is essential as you progress up the career ladder, audition for jobs, and turn your potential for mastery into true musical ability as a performer.

Performers also suggested that you must be able to get along with others, particularly other performers, conductors, and administrators. You must also be able to deal well with artsy personalities and the diva stereotypes. While most performers possess the people skills that were already discussed, there are some performers who place themselves in an elevated status because of their musical accomplishments. As a result, there are situations in which you must be able to deal with fragile egos and the underlying politics that may exist in some performance organizations.

You also need to be flexible, open-minded, intelligent, and creative. As a performer, you may have a specific interpretation of a piece that you have performed many times. An employer with a different approach may ask you to spontaneously change your interpretation to match his or her own. Therefore, you must not only be personally flexible to put your own agenda aside, you must also be musically flexible to perform in a style that may conflict with your own interpretation. This also requires you to have a certain level of intelligence and creativity to know how to manipulate the music in the appropriate manner to meet the desired goal.

You must also be reliable, and this reliability must encompass multiple levels of your personality and musicality. First, you must consistently arrive at rehearsals, performances, recording sessions, and other functions on time, warmed up, in place, and ready to perform when needed. Reliability also means that your part is rehearsed and you do not spend the conductor's time trying to work through difficult passages in your music. Finally, reliability implies that you perform well on a consistent basis.

Finally, returning to the notion that many performers forge their own career paths, you need to have an entrepreneurial mind-set and be capable of promoting yourself as a performing musician. This will require you to be forthcoming and creative and to have a strong personality. This also requires you to be willing to take risks and be innovative in your marketing approach.

SIX

Bachelor of Music in Music Theory

The music theory career field is not well known, especially among high school music students. While there are some high schools that offer music theory classes, most student musicians do not experience music theory until their first year of college. Therefore, many music students come to college with other career goals but change their plans once they are exposed to required theory courses and discover they have a natural ability and interest in music theory.

Most simply stated, a theorist is a musician who analyzes musical compositions to discover how they are written and why they sound the way they do. Theorists use this information to identify similarities and differences among music of different composers or styles. Theorists also identify commonly accepted musical patterns or forms that differentiate one type of composition from another.

Theorists also analyze music from a historical standpoint, looking for differences among music from various time periods and composers within each time period. For example, theorists have worked with music historians to identify the development of fugues in the baroque era, symphonies in the classical era, and twelve-tone music in the twentieth century. Modern-day theorists may also identify innovative techniques of present-day music that may one day be commonly accepted means of composition.

A final and perhaps most common task of music theorists is to help other people understand music better. Theorists work with composers or performers who are struggling to complete or understand a work of music, answering their questions and helping them progress with the piece. Theorists also teach theory in high schools and colleges to help young musicians understand scales, key signatures, meter, and other basic musical elements.

It is difficult to find a musician who is exclusively a music theorist. Theorists spend most of their time teaching, composing, conducting, or performing, or are involved with some other professional aspect of music in addition to fulfilling their interests in theory. Specifically, most music theorists compose or teach theory at the college level and may also teach composition, ear training, or music history. Many universities, in fact, offer only a joint degree in theory and composition, so you may experience difficulty finding a university offering a degree that is distinctly theory. As a result, you may experience equal difficulty finding a career that is related solely to music theory.

CAREER ENTRY

Because most of the careers available in theory involve teaching at the college level, a graduate-level degree is typically required. You may also need to consider that some theorists work in large universities and teach only theory classes. Others at smaller universities teach theory in addition to private lessons, ensemble conducting, or other areas of specialization.

This suggests that while there are musicians who specialize exclusively in theory, there are others with performance, composition, education, or other backgrounds who may have minored in theory or taken additional theory classes. If you are interested in a career in theory but also have other interests, you will most likely be able to simultaneously fulfill both professional goals.

THE JOBS

As stated, the most common career in music theory is teaching at the college level. Theorists are also employed by music publishing companies to edit music. In addition, many theorists compose and arrange music either independently or as university-level composers and composition teachers. Some people with theory degrees have also found jobs teaching piano or other instrument lessons. There are also a number of high school music programs that offer Advanced Placement theory courses, indicating that high school band, choir, and orchestra directors may have additional interests in music theory.

MOST PROMISING LOCATIONS

The most promising locations depend on the job you want to have. If you want to teach theory exclusively, you need to be in a large city with a well-established university music department. For this, you would need to have a doctorate in hand before you begin looking for employment. If you are interested in other areas of music, you may be able to work in a smaller university or in the public school system teaching theory in addition to your other professional duties.

WHAT DOES IT TAKE TO BE A GOOD FIT IN MUSIC THEORY?

Musical Skills

First and foremost, theorists must be able to analyze music. This means that you must have an extensive knowledge of intervals, modalities, tonalities, chord structures, forms, and all other aspects of music. You must also possess the skills to identify these elements in a variety of musical styles and time periods.

Theorists are often expected to identify certain aspects of music without looking at the written notation. Other times, theorists may be expected to sight-read a piece of music for a composer, performer, or group of theory students. Therefore, you must have a well-developed musical ear and the ability to aurally identify musical elements. Your aural skills must be matched by an equally developed skill in sight-reading.

Composition skills are also beneficial for theorists as these skills help theorists understand musical compositions at a deeper level. Composition skills are also necessary because many theorists are also composers. And, as composition commonly begins at the keyboard, theorists must be able to play the piano at a high level in addition to having performance ability in their primary area.

Because compositional techniques were developed over the course of many years, music theorists must possess an extensive knowledge of music history. This knowledge helps theorists identify compositional forms, patterns, and other aspects that were unique to each time period throughout musical development.

Nonmusical Skills

Theorists usually spend a majority of their time teaching. Therefore, many of the skills needed for professional music educators are the same skills required of theorists. Specifically, theorists must have strong communication skills as they relate their skills and knowledge to other musicians. Theorists must also have strong interpersonal, or people, skills.

Critical thinking is also an essential nonmusical skill for music theorists. Many times, there are multiple answers to the same question pertaining to music analysis. Also, the most notable composers throughout music history were notorious for bending rules, breaking rules, and inventing their own rules. Therefore, analyzing a musical example from an innovative composer requires the ability to think outside the box.

Finally, theorists commonly teach, perform, analyze, and compose using a variety of musical software and hardware applications. Music technology has also been a common compositional tool since the early twentieth century, creating a need for theorists to understand how technology is used to create certain musical sounds and to manipulate the sounds of traditional musical instruments. Therefore, theorists must be adept at using music technology and remain current on the most up-to-date technological applications pertaining to music.

Musical Interests

Music theorists are naturally interested in the way music works and how it is put together. They enjoy dissecting a piece of music, analyzing how each individual component contributes to the overall composition. This interest is closely linked to the analytical mind that was discussed earlier. This also indicates why theorists are naturally interested in composition. An analysis of a musical composition may lead to a new discovery that theorists may eventually use in their own original works.

Nonmusical Interests

There are strong relationships between music theory and math. This relationship may be as basic as the fractional value of rhythmic notation or the intervallic relationships between pitches, or as deep as the mathematical patterns used by Mozart and many other composers in their works. Therefore, theorists typically express interests in math and analytical tasks.

Theorists are also commonly interested in teaching. A career as a theory teacher may be a suitable option for musicians who do not see themselves teaching general music or directing high school ensembles. However, as was stated earlier, because most theorists teach at the college level, a graduate degree is required.

Musical Work Values (How You Feel Musically Rewarded)

In music theory, there is a sense of career stability that may not exist in performance or other areas of music. Because theory is considered a fundamental skill of basic musicianship, there will always be a need for theory teachers in colleges, universities, and some secondary schools. Innovations in composition techniques also lead to a continuous need for theorists to analyze new compositions, so there will also be a need for theorists in other professional capacities. As a result, theorists state that they feel rewarded by the sense of career stability and the ability to stay involved with music.

Theorists also suggest that they feel rewarded by teaching and by helping other people understand music better. Teaching enables theorists to work with talented performers and remain active in their own creative and musical endeavors. In many cases, teaching someone else to understand music enables theorists to increase their own understanding of music.

Work Values (How You Feel Personally or Professionally Rewarded)

Music theorists state that they feel professionally rewarded by the ability to teach at the college level. Because music theory is considered a basic skill for all music degree programs, there is a steady need for music theory teachers in university music programs. Teaching at the college level also enables theorists to use music theory to improve their own performances and to stay involved in a field that they love.

Personal Characteristics

It is noted earlier in this chapter that music theory is a very analytical field. Therefore, as a theorist, you need to be intelligent and inquisitive as you seek to answer various questions about music. Music theory also requires a good bit of creativity as you will frequently be asked to think outside the box while analyzing music of avant-garde composers.

As a theorist, you may also be required to spend hours at a time secluded in a studio, analyzing a piece of music. Therefore, you need to be able to concentrate on a singular task for long periods of time. In addition, a good bit of autonomy or self-initiative is beneficial for the completion of tedious tasks commonly required of music theorists. Finally, because you will spend a great deal of time studying music and helping other musicians understand it better, it is crucial that you love music.

The last group of personal characteristics pertains mainly to theorists' role as teachers. In any profession where you might teach music theory, you need to be a strong communicator, enthusiastic, and open minded. You need to be approachable and understanding of those who may not understand theory as well as you. You also need to be able to relate music theory to other musical disciplines as you will spend a majority of your time working with performers, composers, and other musicians who need to understand how theory relates to them.

SEVEN

Bachelor of Music in Composition

In the previous chapter, it is noted that most music theorists also compose or perform other musical tasks. Similarly, it is difficult to find composers who are not also theorists or performers, or who are not involved in some other aspect of music on a professional level. Most composers teach theory at the college level, conduct, perform, or work in some other professional capacity as a musician.

Specifically, composers may perform, work in church music positions, or conduct ensembles while also working as composers. Many composers also teach in a secondary area such as theory or applied lessons in addition to composing. Therefore, if you are interested in pursuing a career in composition, you may benefit from a variety of supplemental classes including conducting, music education, or pedagogy, in addition to the required composition curriculum.

Also, the term *composer* is an incredibly vague label and can imply everything from a composer of symphonies, operas, and works for symphonic bands, to a composer of popular music, songwriter, or composer of commercial jingles and movie sound tracks. As of this writing, there is also a growing market for musicians who compose for websites and video game companies.

Because there is such diversity in the types of music in which composers may specialize, there is equal diversity in the type of undergraduate degrees that may lead to a career in composition. If you want to compose serious music or art music, the terms commonly used for symphonic, orchestral, or choral literature, you may need to pursue a degree in theory and/or composition. Musicians who want to compose the other types of music listed previously may prefer to pursue a degree in music business with an emphasis in composition, as these genres are more commonly associated with popular or commercial composition.

CAREER ENTRY

Like many other careers in music, there are two common paths for career entry into the field of composition. The fields of popular songwriting and commercial music are open to anyone with the necessary skills and therefore no degree may be required. If, however, you want to teach composition at the college level, a graduate degree is usually required. Even in fields where a degree may be considered optional, professional musicians strongly recommend that you receive formal training in the tools, techniques, and processes of music composition.

THE JOBS

Many of the jobs for musicians interested in composition may be more accurately described as areas of specialization rather than jobs. Specifically, composers usually specialize in concert music or art music, video game music, commercial jingles, music for television and films, theme parks, or Broadway-style music. Also, while some composers specialize in one genre, others compose in multiple formats and for a variety of performing organizations.

Regarding the types of jobs that are available to composers, each area of specialization may lead to a different type of employment. Some composers of art music serve as composers in residence for professional ensembles or universities. Most composers teach theory and composition classes at the college level. Composers may also work as engravers, editors, or proofreaders at music publishing companies; work as administrators for performing ensembles or organizations; conduct an ensemble; or work as producers for publishing or recording companies. Some composers also work as freelance performers to supplement their income.

MOST PROMISING LOCATIONS

Like most jobs in music, the most promising locations are determined primarily by the type of career you wish to pursue. If you wish to compose music for film and television, it is most beneficial to move to Los Angeles or New York, where a majority of movies and shows are filmed and where there is an abundant number of recording studios. Composers of popular music may need to live close to Nashville, where their music will be more accessible to recording company executives. Composers who want to work for publishing companies or teach at the college level need to be willing to move to the city where they are offered a job.

WHAT DOES IT TAKE TO BE A GOOD FIT IN COMPOSITION?

Musical Skills

To be a good composer, you need to be a strong performer in your primary area. This ability will give you a better understanding of the performance demands of your compositions. You need to have a thorough knowledge of theory, aural skills, orchestration, and counterpoint to ensure your music adheres to commonly accepted musical guidelines and structures. You need to have a general knowledge of a variety of musical instruments so you will know the limitations and techniques of each instrument for which you compose.

Knowledge of multiple musical styles and time periods is also essential as you may be expected to compose in the style of various historical or modern composers. It is also helpful if you have at least some ability at the piano as many composers use the piano to sound out melodies and harmonies before assigning them to various instruments.

Since the early twentieth century, technology has had a profound impact on music. Technology has allowed composers to manipulate the sounds of traditional instruments and create new, digital instruments with their own distinct timbres. In many circles, technology has also replaced pen-and-paper composition as many composers now use one of the commercial notation software packages to write their music. Therefore, you need to have a strong grasp of technology and the many facets of technology that pertain to music.

Nonmusical Skills

First, composers must have excellent people skills to fulfill their professional obligations. Composers frequently work with administrators and donors who have commissioned a piece of music to ascertain the specifics of the requested piece. Composers also work with conductors and performers in the process of preparing a new piece for a premiere performance. Finally, composers are commonly asked to introduce their music to audience members at preconcert presentations and receptions. In each of these examples, people skills are essential to the success of a career in composition.

Many composers also market their newly released and forthcoming music to performers, conductors, and publishing companies, so that their new works can be premiered, recorded, and sold. For success in these tasks, composers need to have excellent entrepreneurial skills, organization, and business acumen.

Finally, composition requires a great deal of analytical thought. Some composers also rely on mathematical computations as the basis for their compositions. Therefore, composers need to have an analytical mind and a general knowledge of mathematics.

Musical Interests

Most composers gained their initial exposure to music through their experiences in high school performing ensembles. Later in their formal training, they learned of their deeper interest in creating new music and expressing themselves through their compositions. In general, composers are also interested in the processes and techniques of creating music, and in the development of compositional forms over time.

Many composers are also very interested in discussing their works with other composers as a means of generating new ideas and improving in their compositional skills. Composers also express a general love of all types of music and draw on a diverse range of musical examples for compositional ideas. Next, composers enjoy collaborating with performers in the process of creating new pieces to ensure their music meets performers' needs and audience expectations.

Nonmusical Interests

Composers frequently suggest that the inspiration for their compositions comes from their interactions with nonmusical hobbies and interests. Therefore, most composers suggest that you try to have a broad array of nonmusical interest. As a rule, most composers are interested in visual arts, poetry, theater, history, religion, psychology, and philosophy.

Musical Work Values (How You Feel Musically Rewarded)

Composers feel rewarded as much by the process of composition as they do by the product, or the final work. They enjoy hearing their music performed at a high level and receiving audience feedback. They feel rewarded by collaborating with talented performers and conductors to produce a quality work, and they feel rewarded by pushing themselves to consistently improve as musicians.

Nonmusical Work Values (How You Feel Personally or Professionally Rewarded)

Composers also feel rewarded by peer recognition and accolades. They feel rewarded when performers desire to learn their music, and they enjoy working with performers in the process of preparing for performances. They feel rewarded when they experience the world premiere of their latest compositions and see the fruits of months or years of hard work.

Lastly, composers state that they feel rewarded by getting paid to do what they love. Because many composers spend a lot of time doing other things, they may feel an extra sense of satisfaction when they reach a point in their careers when they can support themselves through their compositions, rather than teaching, performing, or working in a nonmusical job.

Personal Characteristics

In one specific aspect, becoming a composer is quite dissimilar to becoming a teacher or performer. As a performer, you can be certain that every large ensemble employs a certain number of performers and that any number of positions may be available from year to year. Likewise, career stability as a music teacher is found in knowing that most schools employ at least a part-time music teacher and that jobs are usually available on a regular basis.

There are not many professional organizations, however, that maintain a full-time staff composer. Therefore, to be a good fit in a composition career, you need have strong determination and tenacity to seek employment and support yourself during periods of unemployment. You also need to be a collegial person, able to deal with a variety of musical stereotypes, including the cantankerous conductor and the diva.

You need to be a good communicator to help conductors and performers understand the intention of your compositions. You may also be asked to introduce your works to an audience before a premiere performance or host receptions following the concert, again emphasizing the need for good people and communication skills.

As a composer, you need to be willing to take risks as the most noted composers throughout history were those who pushed the boundaries. You also need to be open to new ideas as they may become the inspiration for your next masterpiece. An excellent sense of creativity and imagination will also enable you to compose music that does not sound like mere recreations of previously composed music.

Composition can sometimes be a very tedious task. One day, you may finish an entire piece in a few hours, while the next day yields only the completion of a measure or two. As such, you need to be well disciplined and able to work for long periods of time without supervision and without distraction. You may also experience circumstances where your piece must be delivered to a publisher or performer by a certain deadline. You must therefore be reliable to complete your compositions in a timely manner.

You also need to know generally what sounds good concerning new compositions. This pertains both to your ability to evaluate new music of other composers and to recognize the musical value of your own compositions. This ability will enable you to build on aspects of your music that are worthy of your time, and of your audience members, and minimize or eliminate elements that are not.

Next, composers who have reached a certain status and whose works are performed throughout the world are commonly requested to coach an ensemble that is preparing a premiere performance of a new work or to introduce new music to an audience at a premiere concert. Therefore, you need to be flexible and willing to travel, especially as your music grows in popularity. You may also be expected to organize a tour of your own to promote your new music to publishing companies and performing organizations.

Lastly, as a composer, you must be able to accept criticism, and this criticism may come from multiple directions at any given time. Performers may not like a melody or agree with your phrasing suggestions. Conductors may not agree with your interpretation or dynamic marking. A music critic may not like your instrumentation or libretto. You may receive multiple rejection letters from publishers before you find a publisher who will buy your music. In all these scenarios, you must be able to deal with negativity concerning your work.

EIGHT

Bachelor of Music in Music History and Literature

Music history and literature is perhaps the least well-known grouping of music careers. Many of the commonly used career-advising websites, books, and other databases do not even list music history and literature as a career option. Furthermore, there are few people, even among trained musicians, who are aware of the extent of careers available in music history. Regardless, there is a wide variety of careers in music history and literature (musicology) for interested musicians. There are also related careers in the field of ethnomusicology, the study of music from across the world.

The most likely career in music history and literature is teaching at the university level. At this level, it is generally accepted that the study of music history refers specifically to the music of Mozart, Beethoven, and the other common composers from Western Europe and America. This study also includes the related musical, literary, and artistic movements or styles from ancient times to the twenty-first century. However, there are really four distinct categories, or areas of specialization, within the field of music history.

The term *art music* refers to the musical genres of the previously mentioned composers, styles, and time periods. Most musicologists have a broad-based knowledge of music history and then specialize in one particular time period or one composer from that time period. Some university music departments host collegium ensembles where performers use historically accurate instruments. In these ensembles, musicologists may also specialize in one particular instrument from music history.

Almost all university music programs require music majors to enroll in at least two to four semesters of music history courses that focus solely on the study of art music. Musicologists at the university level are expected to teach these undergraduate- and graduate-level courses, and to research and write books and journal articles in their area of specialization. Therefore, there may be the greatest number of job openings in this field of musicology.

Second, there are musicologists whose primary focus is the study of popular or commercial music genres. These include rock, pop, rap, country, hip-hop, and multiple other styles, as well as the music composed for video games, commercials, television shows, and movies. These genres may also focus more intently on digital music media in addition to traditional instruments and ensembles. This specialization may be more common in larger universities and music departments with a commercial music or music business degree.

The next area of specialization is called *ethnomusicology*, or the study of music of non-Western European traditions. Most ethnomusicologists study a wide array of musical styles and genres from across the world, and then specialize in the music of one particular country or ethnic group. Many also specialize in one particular instrument or vocal technique.

Lastly, some musicologists focus solely on one or more of the multiple genres of jazz music. In this specialization, there may be some crossover in the job description of a jazz-musicologist and a musician with a degree in jazz studies (discussed later in this book). The primary difference between the two is that a jazz studies degree focuses mainly on the performance of jazz music, while a musicological study of jazz focuses more on research of, listening to, and writing about jazz genres. It is also common to find musicians who consider themselves as both performers and researchers, or ethnomusicologists, of jazz music.

This scenario reveals additional connections of musicology careers into other areas of music. A musician with a musicology background may be hired to research and write program notes for a performance organization, and may also perform in one or more of the organization's primary ensembles. It is also common for musicians in these roles to move into administrative positions later in their careers. In situations such as these, a musician may be considered a musicologist and a music business professional, while maintaining at least part-time status as an ensemble performer.

Through these scenarios, it becomes evident that there is quite an array of professional opportunities for musicologists and ethnomusicologists. In short, there are some jobs where musicologists may work solely as music historians, either researching or teaching, and other jobs where musicologists may perform other professional duties in addition to teaching or researching music history.

CAREER ENTRY

Because a majority of the careers in musicology are related to teaching at the college level, a degree in music is usually required. Specifically, teaching at the college level requires at least a master's degree, and usually a doctorate. In other areas where musicologists may be employed, a college degree may be desired but not required.

In these types of careers, musicians spend a great deal of time researching and writing about music. Therefore, musicians may benefit from a degree in English or journalism in addition to or in lieu of a music degree. In general, some careers may be available in musicology to people without a degree, but the options are considerably limited.

THE JOBS

The most common career in the field of music history and literature is teaching at the college level. Musicologists also commonly work as music critics for newspapers, magazines, or other journals. A music critic attends concerts and writes reviews of the performances, of the performers, and sometimes of new compositions premiered at an event.

Musicologists also work as program note annotators or authors of books about music history. As a program note annotator, musicologists research information about the musical selections of an upcoming performance and write short articles that will be distributed to audience members at the performance or inserted in the concert program.

Musicologists also work as arts administrators or music advisors for record companies, radio stations, television stations, or work independently as music consultants. In these roles, musicologists work with other staff members to select music for an upcoming event, program, or other publicly broadcast show. Some musicologists are also music editors or orchestra librarians or work in radio broadcast. As before, these musicologists play key roles in selecting appropriate music for an event or performance.

MOST PROMISING LOCATIONS

As with many other music careers, the most promising locations for musicology careers depends on the type of career you wish to pursue. Any college with a medium to large music department will hire musicologists. At smaller colleges, the musicologist may also teach other classes, private lessons, or have release time to maintain a part-time performing career. If you wish to work with a professional ensemble as a program note annotator or critic, you need to move to a large city with a variety of performance venues, or large newspapers that hire music critics.

WHAT DOES IT TAKE TO BE A GOOD FIT IN
MUSIC HISTORY AND LITERATURE?

Musical Skills

To pursue a career in musicology, you need to be strong in theory, analysis, and score reading as these skills will contribute to your ability to write about music. It is also helpful if you are a competent performer, have some piano ability, and have conducting experience. You also need a thorough knowledge of compositional techniques, systems of musical notation from all periods of music history, and the ways in which instruments were used in various historical periods. It is also helpful if you have good aural skills and sight-singing ability.

Nonmusical Skills

Musical development throughout history is closely linked to political leaders, literary and artistic movements, and even to architectural developments that have occurred. Therefore, to become a successful musicologist, you need a thorough knowledge of world history, visual arts, world literature, philosophy, and church history.

As most of the world's well-known art music was written in countries whose native language is not English, you need to have at least a rudimentary competency in multiple languages. This is especially the case for ethnomusicologists whose primary duties involve music of culture groups from around the world.

Similarly, as a musicologist you may spend as much time reading about music as you spend reading the music itself. Therefore, you need to have good reading comprehension skills, excellent research skills, and critical thinking skills.

More so, because the point of your research will be to pass new information along to other people, you need to have excellent writing skills, public speaking and teaching ability, and people skills. The latter are especially important for musicologists who teach music history or related courses.

Musical Interests

To be a good fit in a musicology career, you should have interests in a variety of musical genres and the historical performance practice of music. As you learn about a broad range of music, you may also develop a specific interest in a particular composer, genre, or time period. Many musicologists specialize in a particular instrument, instrument family, or voice concentration, so you may be a good fit if you are interested in the historical development of a particular instrument, vocal technique, or vocal style. Finally, as you will spend a great deal of time listening to music, you need to have a strong interest in listening to and transcribing music.

Nonmusical Interests

The study of music history delves deeply into the study of other areas, particularly how those areas have related to music throughout the ages. Therefore, you need to have an interest in history, sociology, literature, theology, and visual arts. Musicologists also do extensive research in aesthetics, anthropology, and the use of technology in music.

Musical Work Values (How You Feel Musically Rewarded)

Musicologists are commonly inquisitive people who enjoy research and sharing their research with others. Musicologists feel rewarded by their ability to answer other people's questions about music and the ability to answer their own questions pertaining to music. They also feel rewarded by performing music of all time periods on instruments that were used when the music was composed and by learning to understand the relationships between modern genres and music from various historical time periods.

Nonmusical Work Values (How You Feel Personally or Professionally Rewarded)

Musicologists feel rewarded by sharing their research and ideas, and by helping other people understand music on a deeper level. They also enjoy helping other people understand the connections between all arts, as well as the role of music in all cultures. In addition, a musicologist's research commonly leads him or her to places of importance around the world. Therefore, you will be a good fit in a musicology career if you feel rewarded by the opportunity to travel.

Personal Characteristics

Like most other music careers, you will be a good fit in musicology if you have a very strong work ethic and are able to work for extended periods of time without supervision, direction, or interruption from others. It is helpful if you are inquisitive, intelligent, can think logically about a variety of problems and research topics, are detail oriented, and enjoy reading. Finally, you need to be patient, flexible, and open minded, particularly when dealing with students. It also helps to have a sense of humor and people skills.

NINE

Bachelor of Music in Sacred Music

The term *sacred music* applies to any career wherein you lead music in a place of worship. Professionals in this career field are sometimes referred to as worship pastors, music directors, music ministers, cantors, or song leaders. While many assume that the term *sacred* refers only to Catholic and Protestant practices, it is important to remember that most religions around the world uphold their own musical traditions. Therefore, the sacred music career field is not limited to any particular religion or denomination.

As a church musician, your primary responsibility is twofold. First, you must prepare the music that will be included in the weekly worship service. This may involve teaching a new piece to a choir; working with a pianist, organist, or other instrumental ensemble of some kind; or simply selecting the music that you will lead as a soloist.

The second aspect of this job is the more visible component. Once you select and prepare music with the other performing soloists or ensembles in your place of worship, you must lead the congregation in worship, share the music you prepared during the week, and generally, help a gathering of nonmusicians participate with music, usually through singing.

As of this writing, sacred music careers in many denominations are in a very noticeable state of transition. Previously, as a sacred musician or church musician, you would be expected to conduct a choir, perhaps play piano or organ, and be able to conduct an orchestra or instrumental ensemble. In current trends, however, many denominations are moving away from this model and increasingly use music with more of a popular, perhaps untrained sound. Therefore, church musicians may need more training in guitar, sound equipment, and songwriting and arranging, rather than choral conducting and the other skills previously mentioned.

Furthermore, whereas previous generations of church musicians needed extensive knowledge of hymns and church music liturgy, current models rely more on praise choruses and songs from Christian radio during worship services, primarily in Protestant denominations. Although these trends are growing in popularity, there are still a number of congregations and denominations that hold true to traditional styles of worship in their weekly services.

Therefore, it is important for you to research not only the type of church or place of worship in which you want to work, but also the beliefs of the faculty members in the university you plan to attend. Specifically, ensure that the training you will receive is in philosophical alignment with the type of career you wish to pursue.

CAREER ENTRY

Because of recent trends discussed in the previous paragraphs, there are many careers in sacred music that may be available to musicians who do not have a college degree. Specifically, smaller congregations and those who want more of a contemporary sound may be more likely to hire a music leader without formal training in music.

In situations such as these, it may be more common for the church to hire someone from within the congregation or someone whose religious and philosophical beliefs are in alignment with those of the denomination. Most sacred musicians agree that there is no control over who a church hires. Therefore, there is not a lot of standardization concerning requirements for career entry.

THE JOBS

In addition to working as a church music director, musicians with a degree in sacred music may be employed in a number of different areas. Some musicians are hired by larger congregations as church organists, piano accompanists, or other instrumental performers. Larger congregations also hire musicians to work with specific ensembles such as hand bell ensembles or children's choirs.

Sacred musicians also compose or arrange music for churches, or may work in music publishing companies that specialize in sacred music. It is also common for sacred musicians to work in denominational offices as music administrators for groups of churches in their area or to join a missions organization to travel across the world to lead music in a foreign church.

Finally, musicians with a sacred music background may also be performers in contemporary religious bands or may teach in university sacred music programs. As with other career fields, teaching sacred music at the university level requires a graduate degree, usually in sacred music.

MOST PROMISING LOCATIONS

The specification of most promising locations does not really apply to this music career field. Even the smallest, most isolated communities will have places of worship that employ at least a part-time music leader. In some small churches, the music leader may also work as the pastor or youth director, or perform some other function in the church, and may also have a different job during the week. As with most other careers in music, you have to decide where you want to live and the type of church in which you want to work.

A primary determination for this career may be more directly related to your particular religion or denomination. Jewish synagogues and Muslim mosques, for example, are more common in larger suburban or urban settings than in rural communities. Even within certain denominations, there are regional differences that impact the type of music used in the church. For example, Baptist churches may be Southern Baptist, North American Baptist, Independent Baptist, or a number of other variations, each with its own musical expectations.

WHAT DOES IT TAKE TO BE A GOOD FIT IN SACRED MUSIC?

Musical Skills

Because church musicians lead congregations in music on a weekly basis, you must first be a strong performer in your primary area (usually keyboard, guitar, and voice). You also need good conducting skill, both in a traditional choral setting and in contemporary styles. It is helpful if you have strong ear-training/aural skills and are able to read music in multiple clefs.

You need to have a strong knowledge of music theory, composing, and arranging as it is common for church musicians to rewrite music based on the individual needs of their church. Finally, you need to have an extensive knowledge of the traditional music within your denomination and a general knowledge of church music history.

Nonmusical Skills

The primary nonmusical skill for sacred musicians is people skills. Apart from that, you need to be a good communicator and have strong administrative skills. You also need to have a general knowledge of theology, psychology, church history, and various aspects of ministerial life. Finally, as you may be responsible for ordering and maintaining sound equipment for your church, you need to have a general knowledge of sound systems and related technology.

Musical Interests

Music educators suggest that musicians are drawn to their career field because of good experiences in high school performing ensembles. Similarly, many church music directors are led to the career field because of prior experiences in church music. In addition, church musicians state that they are interested in the function of music in a ministry setting.

Nonmusical Interests

Just as music teachers are regarded as both musicians and educators, sacred music professionals are commonly regarded as musicians and pastors, or religious leaders. Therefore, to be a good fit in a sacred music career, you need to have a general interest in religion, theology, and life in ministry. It is also beneficial if you are interested in working with people on a daily basis. While you may lead a congregation in music only one day each week, there are additional facets of the job that will require you to work with people on a regular basis.

Finally, church musicians commonly express that they feel a sense of calling to the profession. Sacred musicians suggest that there are two additional traits that must accompany one's calling: open-mindedness and flexibility. Some may feel called to the profession but may not know why they feel called or to what specific capacity they feel called. There are also some students who declare they feel called to a specific type of church music ministry in a specific type of church. According to some church musicians, this type of calling is usually inauthentic. Students with a true sense of calling should also express an open-mindedness to go wherever they are led.

Musical Work Values (How You Feel Musically Rewarded)

Sacred music professionals suggest that they feel rewarded by helping nonmusicians develop their musical skills and by leading a congregation in weekly worship. Sacred musicians enjoy seeing people come together for a musical cause, the time spent in rehearsal, and the ability to rehearse and perform a wide variety of music.

Nonmusical Work Values (How You Feel Personally or Professionally Rewarded)

According to sacred music professionals, both church musicians and music educators spend a majority of their professional time helping non-musical people feel successful in musical endeavors. Accordingly, sacred music professionals feel most rewarded by helping others feel successful at musical tasks.

Other sacred music professionals suggest that people do not enter this career field for their own rewards, but so that other people may come closer to God or another deity through their musical efforts. Some do, however, suggest that they feel rewarded by a sense of appreciation for their work and by a feeling of community generated in rehearsals and performances.

Personal Characteristics

The most desirable personality trait for sacred music professionals is humility. In this career field, you will work primarily with volunteers who may resent a music director with an air of superiority or arrogance. This is especially true because a majority of your volunteers will be musi-cally untrained people and may feel threatened by a director who lacks humility.

In addition to humility, you must be a people person, possess a desire to serve others, and be a strong leader. In any large gathering of people, you will experience a variety of personalities, some of which may be quite difficult or problematic. Leadership skills are crucial in directing such a diverse group of individuals toward a common goal of preparing music for a weekly service.

Similarly, you must have an outgoing personality, a positive outlook, and a sense of humor. These traits will enable you to recruit additional volunteers and to maintain people who already participate in your pro-gram. Just as volunteers will not want to work with a director who lacks leadership skills, they will simply stop coming if the director is dull or lifeless or brings no energy to the rehearsals or performances.

You need to have a strong work ethic and a good stage presence. A positive work ethic will enable you to handle multiple tasks at one time and to maintain a schedule that can become quite grueling during certain times of the year. A good stage presence is also vital as you will spend a great deal of time in front of people, either rehearsing ensembles or lead-ing congregations in music.

Next, it is common in many churches for the spiritual leader to select a given topic or theme for the weekly sermon, and ask the music director to select music that is related to the theme. Some staff members may also have their own view of the overall purpose of music in the church and expect you to adhere to their stated expectations. In these circumstances, you must be flexible, open-minded, selfless, and willing to submit to the leadership of the church. You must also be well educated so that you will be able to find suitable music that meets the requirements described by your superiors.

Finally, you must have a strong personal faith and devotion to God. As stated before, while you are primarily a musician, you are also a staff member of your place of worship and will be viewed accordingly by members of your congregation. There may also be a variety of undesirable circumstances, as there are with any job, that may make you question your career choice. Your devotion to God and your sense of calling to the career are vital traits to help you through potentially troublesome situations.

TEN

Bachelor of Music in Jazz Studies

Jazz studies is a very broad career field encompassing an equally diverse grouping of musical genres. Over time, jazz music has come to include big band, swing, cool, funk, blues, bebop, and a number of additional jazz subgenres. There is also a great deal of crossover into rock and other popular genres, and into musical genres from other cultures. As such, jazz musicians may work in any number of environments and perform in a variety of different musical styles.

The jazz studies career field can also be closely compared to the performance career field. While those who major in performance will work their way into symphony orchestras, opera companies, and other concert halls, jazz musicians work their way into jazz clubs, nightclubs, touring jazz ensembles, and recording studios. Some may also eventually perform in rock or other popular music ensembles, or may focus on jazz music of other countries.

Just as in performance, many jazz musicians survive by piecing together a number of part-time performance opportunities and may also work in nonmusical jobs to support their performance endeavors. Jazz musicians may also be expected to perform at least part-time in other genres including show bands, orchestral work, or studio work.

The primary differences between performance and jazz studies include the types of instruments on which musicians perform, the manner in which the instruments are used, and the vocal styles that are implemented. The differences between a lead trumpet player in a swing band and a principal trumpet in an orchestra, for example, may be akin to the differences between a fiddle player in a bluegrass band and a concert violinist. While there are obvious similarities, they are usually overshadowed by the differences in performance technique and overall sound.

There are also stark contrasts between the types of ensembles in performance and jazz studies, and the performance venues and musical genres in which musicians may work. While a concert violinist may perform in a tuxedo on a large concert stage, a jazz musician may perform in a nightclub wearing casual attire. There are also a number of exclusive restaurants and dinner clubs that hire jazz musicians to perform in very upscale environments.

Because of the diverse nature of jazz music, and the venues in which jazz music is performed, there is a vast assortment of careers available to jazz musicians. As you read the following information, bear in mind that some aspects are more or less applicable based on your instrument, voice type, or particular career interests. Other pieces of information, however, are essential in any career in jazz studies, regardless of any particular specialization.

CAREER ENTRY

According to the jazz musicians who were interviewed for this book, any of the career opportunities in jazz studies may be available to musicians who do not have a college degree. There are even a small handful of university professors in jazz studies who do not hold college degrees. As a caveat, these musicians work primarily in private conservatories and have extensive experience, exceptional skill, and outstanding reputations in their fields. Even still, a university's ability to hire nondegreed faculty members is quickly becoming an outdated model as new regulations for colleges and universities require faculty to hold graduate degrees.

Although the degree is not required in other jazz studies careers, professionals in the field strongly recommend that all musicians who wish to enter the career field pursue a degree. The formal training and professional network gained through the process of obtaining a degree in music is an invaluable asset to those who wish to become jazz musicians. Also, like performance careers, there are many more jazz musicians than there are full-time jobs in the field. The degree provides additional training and network opportunities that may lead to employment more quickly than seeking a job without the degree.

THE JOBS

As is stated earlier, jazz musicians perform in a wide array of venues. The more common performance opportunities for jazz musicians include recording studios, nightclubs, some restaurants, and concert halls. Jazz musicians may also perform as freelance musicians and band members for various touring performers. It is in these touring ensembles that jazz musicians may commonly be expected to perform in popular or other rock genres in addition to their work as jazz musicians.

It is also common for jazz musicians to have a number of part-time performance engagements and to perform in more than one type of ensemble. Some jazz musicians, particularly those who play woodwind instruments (saxophone, primarily), also play a different instrument in each ensemble or play multiple instruments in one ensemble. It is quite common, for example, for a member of the saxophone section to double on clarinet or flute.

Many jazz musicians also compose and arrange their own music. In addition to performing the standard jazz repertoire at their concerts, these musicians work their original compositions into the set with the hopes of eventually publishing their own record of original music. More commonly, though, jazz musicians rearrange jazz standards into different styles or to fit a different instrumentation than the original score.

There are also opportunities for jazz musicians to teach at the high school or college level, or teach independently. In school settings, jazz musicians lead jazz ensembles, usually in a big-band format, and perhaps also coach a variety of smaller jazz combos. Teaching individually, however, focuses primarily on private lessons, either in vocal or instrumental performance, or in composing and arranging jazz music.

MOST PROMISING LOCATIONS

Most major cities have a variety of performance venues for jazz musicians. There are, however, a number of metropolitan areas that are reputed for an active scene for jazz musicians and a distinctive style of jazz that is unique to the area. Some of the more well-known areas for jazz musicians include New Orleans, Chicago, Detroit, and other large cities.

It is important to note again the incredible diversity of jazz music and the strong relationship of geographical location to preferred jazz style. New Orleans jazz, for instance, is very different than the type of jazz that is performed in a New York City nightclub. Therefore, it is important that you do enough research to know the type of location in which you want to live and the specific type of jazz music you want to perform.

WHAT DOES IT TAKE TO BE A GOOD FIT IN JAZZ STUDIES?

Musical Skills

Because the field of jazz studies is primarily a performance-based career field, you need to have complete mastery of your primary instrument or voice for potential success as a jazz musician. Also, to increase your potential for finding a job, you need to be able to perform in multiple styles of music. It is also crucial that you have a thorough knowledge of jazz literature and are fluent in the vocabulary of jazz music.

Because jazz music relies more stringently on improvisation than other performance genres, you need to be a competent improviser. Your ability to improvise will be greatly enhanced if you have strong sight-reading skills, ear-training ability, a thorough knowledge of music theory, and skill in composing and arranging. Composing and arranging skills will also enable you to perform music in a variety of settings and with different vocal or instrumental ensembles.

Finally, jazz musicians commonly perform on more than one instrument. Therefore, the ability to perform well on a secondary instrument, and possibly piano, is a desirable attribute for jazz musicians.

Nonmusical Skills

Just as in performance careers, there is a large number of jazz musicians competing for a relatively small number of jobs. It is therefore important that you possess the necessary people skills that will enable you to build personal and professional networks that may eventually lead to employment. You also need to have strong entrepreneurial skills, networking skills, communication skills, and professionalism as you promote yourself as a performer.

As many jazz musicians work in a number of part-time careers, it is helpful if you have a working knowledge of music business and organization skill. A basic facility with accounting is also useful to help you manage several part-time incomes and organize your finances. In addition, because many jazz performers also teach, it is helpful if you have some training or ability in pedagogy (teaching).

Next, because there are such close connections between jazz music and the music of other cultures, it is helpful if you have some facility with other languages and knowledge of musical styles from around the world.

Finally, jazz music commonly relies more heavily on technology—namely, sound systems and recording technology, than other performance genres. This is especially the case for performing in large settings and relates primarily to electric guitar, bass, and keyboards. It is therefore essential that you have some facility with technology.

Musical Interests

As is stated earlier, the term *jazz music* is a very ambiguous label that has been applied to many styles of jazz. To be a good fit in a jazz studies career, you need to have a passion for multiple jazz genres and a desire to express yourself through jazz music. Many jazz musicians also state that their initial experiences in high school performing ensembles, particularly jazz bands, led them to pursue a career in jazz studies.

Nonmusical Interests

There is a certain image that surrounds the life and lifestyle of jazz musicians. Many jazz performers state that their interest in the image of jazz music and performance venues led them to pursue a career in jazz studies. Other nonmusical interests include a desire to travel, a desire for variety in one's work, and an interest in how music is produced.

Musical Work Values (How You Feel Musically Rewarded)

Jazz musicians feel most rewarded by the ability to perform with great musicians in a variety of musical styles. They also state that they feel rewarded by the ability to achieve their goals as performing musicians.

Nonmusical Work Values (How You Feel Personally or Professionally Rewarded)

Similar to the musical rewards, jazz musicians feel a sense of personal and professional reward by seeing the fruits of their hard work. This is especially evident when a jazz musician reaches a point in his or her career where he or she no longer has to work multiple jobs, or no longer has to work in a nonmusical job to support him- or herself as a musician.

Jazz musicians also feel rewarded by the ability to participate in the larger community of jazz musicians, the ability to use their skills as performers, and sharing their skills with others. As teachers, jazz musicians also feel rewarded when their students become successful performers.

Personal Characteristics

Like those in other performing careers, jazz musicians suggest that there are significant struggles, particularly for those who are just starting out. Therefore, you need to be very persistent, patient, and self-disciplined.

In addition, as there are more jazz musicians than full-time jobs in jazz music, you need to be reliable, professional, and collegial to build a reputation of good standing in the professional community. You also need to be open minded and willing to learn, as these traits will increase your flexibility and overall knowledge and skill as a performer.

You also need to have a passion for jazz music yet be a well-rounded musician in multiple genres. You also need to be willing to work in a nonmusical job to support yourself as you begin your career. Lastly, you need to be confident and committed to your career as a jazz musician, especially as you encounter the common struggles of early-career performing musicians.

ELEVEN

Bachelor of Music in Pedagogy

The pedagogy career field is very similar to music education in that the primary function of professional musicians in both fields is to teach other people about music. Whereas music education prepares musicians to teach music in private or public school settings, the pedagogy label usually refers to a more precise area of training. Specifically, the term *pedagogy* refers to string and piano teachers who teach group and private lessons, either in their homes, in community music programs, or in music stores that provide teaching spaces.

It is common for pedagogy professionals to seek additional training related to their particular instrument or professional interests. The Suzuki Method, for example, is a common pedagogical approach for string and piano teachers, particularly for younger children. Related curricula and pedagogical approaches also exist for guitar, voice, and many other areas of private music study.

In addition to these instrumental applications of music pedagogy, there are occasional instances of private voice lessons for younger singers, thereby extending pedagogy career opportunities into vocal music. Specifically at the college level, it is common to find courses in vocal pedagogy that prepare singers to teach other people how to sing. However, unlike courses in string and piano pedagogy, vocal pedagogy courses are usually part of other music degree programs and typically do not lead to a career that is devoted solely to teaching.

CAREER ENTRY

One of the musicians interviewed for this book very clearly stated the requirements for career entry into the field of pedagogy: "No one controls who opens up a studio." The point of this statement was to suggest that anybody with an instrument can offer piano or string lessons from their homes regardless of their ability, training, or experience. However, teaching lessons in a formal setting of any kind does typically require a degree.

As a point of clarification and caution, while you may be able to offer lessons even though you may not have the desirable qualifications, there is no guarantee that you will have any interested pupils. More to the point, if parents of student musicians know that you are less qualified than another teacher in town, they will most likely choose the other teacher.

In addition, your ability to teach, your knowledge of the related litera-ture, and your knowledge of student development is directly related to your own training and experience. The more training you have, the more you will be a benefit to your own students. You will also be able to market yourself more as a trained professional and will usually be able to charge a little more for lessons because of additional training. In general, the point of this caution is that while you might be able to teach private lessons without a college degree, this option will significantly limit your potential for success.

THE JOBS

Because the point of a pedagogy degree is to prepare students for teach-ing careers, most of the jobs related to this degree involve teaching piano or strings. As an additional point of clarification, musicians with an edu-cation background are usually labeled as music teachers or band, choir, or orchestra directors. In the pedagogy field, musicians are identified as piano teachers, voice teachers, or other specific instrument teachers. While it may seem restrictive to limit one's title to the teaching of a specific instrument, there is an array of professional opportunities in ped-agogy specifically concerning the settings and student demographics that you may choose to teach.

Specifically, you may choose to teach preschool children, adult learn-ers, or any age group in between. You may teach in your home, in a studio with other instructors, in a day care facility, or in places of wor-ship. You may also find preparatory divisions in some university music programs wherein community children come to a college campus to take music lessons from pedagogy professionals.

Local music stores also commonly rent out practice rooms in the back of the store to teachers who may either teach independently and pay a small facility-use fee to the music store, or may contract directly with the store as a part-time or full-time teacher in their specific area. It may also be common for pedagogy professionals to rent a small facility of their own and teach lessons as a small, independent business.

There is an additional, unique element of careers in pedagogy that does not pertain as directly to other career fields. Private music teachers usually teach students ranging in age from preschool to junior high or high school. As such, most of the teaching time for private lessons is reserved for evenings or weekends, when school-age children are not in class. Therefore, you may find your days a little freer than your evenings and weekends in this field.

In contrast, you are usually freer to determine your own schedule more readily than school music teachers. You have the ability to determine the number of students you wish to teach at a time and when you would like to teach each student, provided that your proposed teaching time does not conflict with school schedules. There is also greater room for flexibility if you need to reschedule lessons for one reason or another.

There is also a recent trend that may extend the potential career opportunities in music pedagogy beyond home and private studios into the public school setting. Specifically, many public schools have begun to offer group piano lessons and Suzuki string classes. Therefore, careers in public school music teaching that have previously been available only to music educators may become available to musicians from other fields— namely, pedagogy.

Other careers that may be available to people with pedagogy degrees include instrument repair technicians, part-time performance, working as a salesperson for an instrument manufacturer or music publisher, or doing editorial work for a music publisher.

MOST PROMISING LOCATIONS

A discussion of most promising locations does not apply to careers in pedagogy as directly as it might to other music career fields. Any small city will have a number of people who want to learn to play piano, guitar, or other instrument. Some small cities will even have a number of places of worship that let local music teachers use a classroom or chapel as a teaching space during the week.

If you want to teach in a formal studio setting, you may need to live in or near a city that is large enough to have a music store or other business property where you could rent teaching space. You would also need to ensure that the city in which you want to live has a large enough population to provide you with enough students to financially sustain you. Lastly, if you choose to live in a smaller community, you would need to be aware of the likelihood of another teacher in town with whom you may compete for students.

There are also teaching opportunities in a large number of colleges or universities that host preparatory divisions or community schools. In these settings, the university music department hires local teachers to teach a variety of lessons and then invites children and other community members to come to the campus for weekly lessons. To teach in this kind of environment, you would need to live near a college that hosts a preparatory division and/or a pedagogy program.

These teaching opportunities are especially good options for college students because universities commonly hire their own music majors as teachers. If the teachers work well in the department, they are usually given the option to keep their teaching position in the community school even after graduating from college. As a point of clarification, these are not considered university faculty positions. They are usually considered staff or contract workers, and are only loosely affiliated with the university.

WHAT DOES IT TAKE TO BE A GOOD FIT IN PEDAGOGY?

Musical Skills

Because the primary responsibility of pedagogy professionals is to teach students how to play an instrument, the most important musical skill in this career field is proficiency at the keyboard or other primary instrument. While performance ability on a primary instrument is an essential musical skill for pedagogy professionals, there is some discrepancy among professional musicians regarding the level of performance ability required in certain career fields—namely, music education and pedagogy. Because this debate is already discussed at length in a previous chapter, it will not be included again here.

There is one peculiar component of this dispute, however, that was not previously discussed and pertains directly to music education and pedagogy. On one hand, you cannot be an excellent teacher unless you are not, first, an excellent musician. On the other hand, there are a large number of musicians who suggest that people who struggled a bit as performers often make the best teachers.

This belief is supported with the justification that musicians who experienced their own difficulties as performers may have a greater sense of empathy for their students, a more finely tuned awareness of problematic aspects of their students' performance, and a greater knowledge of tips and suggestions for overcoming these challenges. Stated simply, musicians who worked through their own struggles may be more successful at helping students conquer their musical issues. These teachers may also know how to motivate and challenge struggling students in a manner that encourages them to mature as musicians rather than generate undue frustration.

Therefore, although proficiency at the keyboard is a common requirement for professionals in music pedagogy, there may also be potential for success in this career field for lesser-skilled performers. This potential is first contingent on the fact that musicians who once struggled have overcome their issues and have progressed to a level of musical proficiency at their primary instrument. This potential for success also assumes that musicians possess the desirable teaching skills that will be described in the next section.

In addition to performance ability, you need to have a good knowledge of the related repertoire for your instrument and have a fundamental knowledge of theory and music history. Because you will occasionally demonstrate the music you select for your students, you need to be a strong sight reader and be able to memorize music well. It is also common for teachers to sing intervals, melodies, or melodic examples for their students, so you must also be a competent singer.

Finally, you need to have good aural skills and be able to identify misplaced notes, incorrect fingerings, poor intonation, and other areas of your students' performances that need correction. You also need to have at least some skill in improvisation. This skill will enable you to demonstrate a variety of musical concepts or skills for your students with little or no time to prepare. It is also common in some curricular approaches for the teacher or student to improvise a melody over a provided chord structure to ensure the student understands the key, meter, chord progression, or related element.

Nonmusical Skills

Because most pedagogy professionals teach a large number of students, you need to be well organized, have a good sense of business skills and marketing, and have a strong sense of professionalism. You also need teaching skills, people skills, empathy for your students, and an ability to understand or relate to your students.

There are also a variety of technological applications that pertain directly to music pedagogy. Piano teachers, for example, commonly teach group lessons of ten to twenty students at a time in digital keyboard labs where the teacher can listen through headphones to individual players, specific groups of players, or the entire class. There are also various software packages that teach students about theory, instrumental fingerings, history, or any number of other aspects. Therefore, you also need to have a working knowledge of music technology related to pedagogy.

Musical Interests

Pedagogy professionals are usually interested in performing and helping other people become better musicians and performers. They also express a general interest in other aspects of their primary instrument. These aspects may include the historical development of their instrument, well-known composers who specialized in their instrument, innovative teaching approaches, technological developments, or any number of related components.

Nonmusical Interests

As musicians in the field of pedagogy are able to work with a diverse range of student demographics and professional environments, you should have a clear idea of the type of student for which you are best suited and should teach primarily or exclusively in that area. Sometimes you may have a clear idea of the age or type of student you want to teach before you begin your career. Other times, it is only after you have taught a particular type of student that you begin to determine your fit. You will also discover that this fit between student and teacher directly impacts your ability to relate to students and teach in a manner most fitting of each student's age and ability.

Other nonmusical interests for careers in pedagogy include the ability to be your own boss, work from home, or arrange your own work schedule. This career field has traditionally appealed to parents of young children who can teach from their homes and do not have to arrange childcare while they work.

While some career fields are prone to encouraging a self-serving mentality among members of the professional community, music pedagogy tends to encourage a focus on other people. Primarily, the focus of pedagogy professionals is usually student growth and fostering a love for music in their students. As this pertains to interests, pedagogy professionals state that their primary interest is in the ability to inspire future generations of musicians.

Musical Work Values (How You Feel Musically Rewarded)

Pedagogy professionals express that they feel most rewarded by sharing music with their students and seeing their students progress as musicians. They also feel rewarded by the appreciation expressed by their students and the parents of those students. The most gratifying event for pedagogy professionals is usually an end-of-year recital where students perform the music they have learned throughout the year for their parents and friends. Additionally, pedagogy professionals feel rewarded when their students continue taking lessons after graduation, perform in college ensembles, or perhaps become professional musicians themselves.

Nonmusical Work Values (How You Feel Personally or Professionally Rewarded)

Pedagogy professionals also feel rewarded by giving other people the tools they need to be successful. They enjoy the sense of community generated between parents, students, and other teachers. Lastly, they enjoy the ability to continue performing and supporting themselves doing what they love.

Personal Characteristics

As in any other career field, there are a variety of professional frustrations with which pedagogy professionals struggle. These musicians work mainly on evenings and weekends when many of their colleagues and friends are at home or off duty. Summer months and holidays usually result in a significant decline of lessons as students leave for vacations, and a decline in lessons results in a decline in income. Therefore, musicians in this field need to very flexible and patient.

You also need to be a good communicator and be able to work well with a variety of personality types. Mainly, you need to be able to communicate your skill and knowledge to your students. You also need to be able to communicate well with parents, encouraging them to get their children to practice, requesting payment when needed, scheduling make-up lessons, or any number of other reasons.

Next, it is important that you be an energetic and motivated person. In this sense, you need to be able to motivate your students to practice, motivate the parents of your students to bring them to lessons on a consistent basis, and motivate yourself to work when many others are at home resting.

Last, you need to be well organized and able to manage a lot of information at one time. Mainly, you will need to keep track of the études, exercises, solos, and other lesson components for each student. You will also be expected to keep track of dates when certain students may need to miss a lesson, and manage payment and attendance records.

TWELVE

Bachelor of Music in Musical Theater

Musical theater is one of the few truly American performance genres. Many of our nation's iconic melodies, songs, characters, and one-liners originated from the scripts of American musical theater. In addition, some of the most noted celebrities in the film industry began their careers in musical theater.

A degree in musical theater prepares you to perform in a number of different venues, with the ultimate goal expressed by many in this field of performing on Broadway. There are also a number of musical theater performers who eventually delve into stage-acting in traditional theater or work their way into movies or television. Some may also transition into careers as opera performers to focus more intently on their singing ability.

Although this is a very common career field, there is little mention of musical theater in many of the standard music career advising publications and online resources. Also, you may find that there are not a lot of university music departments with a distinct musical theater degree. Instead, musical theater is usually a component of either a theater department or a music department that performs musicals on a periodic basis.

This may be because musical theater is labeled a theatrical genre as much as it is labeled a musical genre. Some musicians also view musical theater as a subgenre of opera, when in fact the two are distinctly different. More accurately, musical theater is its own, unique genre, encompassing characteristics of music and theater.

CAREER ENTRY

In most music career fields, there are a number of careers that may be available to musicians without a college degree. This truism is more prevalent in musical theater than in any other music career field. Rather than a music degree, the most important trait for career entry in musical theater is talent. You must be an excellent performer more than anything else. However, a formal training program will prepare you for all aspects of the career field. In addition, a larger percent of university musical theater programs work directly with talent agencies that will keep you up to date concerning auditions and other job opportunities. Therefore, a degree in musical theater or a related field is strongly recommended.

In general, concerning career entry into musical theater, you have two options from which to choose. You can move to New York or another metropolitan area with a large number of musical theater performance venues and find a temporary job while you take as many auditions as you can, hoping to win a coveted position in a performing company. Or you can pursue a degree that will formally train you for the audition process, introduce you to a number of reputable people in the field, and build a professional network that may lead directly to full-time employment in musical theater.

If you choose to pursue a degree in musical theater, you should begin with a thorough research process. Look specifically for universities that have a degree in musical theater and an active musical theater program. If you already know which college you want to attend and have discovered that this college does not have a degree in musical theater, at least check to see that musical theater productions are regularly performed by the theater or music department. You may also want to review the professional bios of the music or theater faculty to ensure that one or more of the professors has a good deal of experience in musical theater.

THE JOBS

The musical theater degree and career field are typically divided into two tracks: performance and design. Performers are usually singers, actors, and dancers who learn Broadway songs and melodies from other well-known show tunes. There are also a number of instrumental performers who play the background or accompanying music for the production (pit musicians), arrange music, and direct the instrumental ensemble during performances.

Musical theater professionals perform on stages in New York City, Los Angeles, Las Vegas, or any number of large cities. Many performers also join professional touring companies, perform on cruise ships or in theme parks, or work as cabaret performers.

There are also a number of musical theater jobs in the design track. These jobs are usually reserved for people who are interested in musical theater but who may be more gifted in one or more of the design areas than as performers. A sampling of the common design careers includes costume design, lighting, sets, and props. A musical theater production also requires technical staff to work as stagehands, run the soundboard during the production, and perform a host of other duties.

There are some musical theater performers who have a stronger background in acting than in singing and therefore may not be able to read music or learn the songs for their part without the help of an accompanist or vocal coach. Coaches are typically people who can play piano and teach singing well enough to help musical theater performers learn their roles.

Musical theater production companies also hire stage managers, administrators, technical directors, and people with business backgrounds in production, marketing, and finance. Some musical theater professionals who are skilled in recognizing talent in other people work as agents or casting directors. Finally, some musical theater performers pursue graduate degrees and teach musical theater at the college level or in high school music/drama programs.

MOST PROMISING LOCATIONS

The best chances for a career in musical theater lie not just on Broadway, but in metropolitan areas with an extensive number of live performance venues devoted to musical theater (New York, Los Angeles, Las Vegas, and Chicago, to name a few). You may also need to look for communities with a larger number of talent agencies that will work with you to find auditions that may be available in locations other than the cities listed previously. As an example, cruise ships usually have large concert halls on board and hire musical theater performers to entertain passengers at sea. There are also extensive employment opportunities in theme parks around the world that hire musical theater performers for seasonal performances.

WHAT DOES IT TAKE TO BE A GOOD FIT IN MUSICAL THEATER?

Musical Skills

As in other performance-based career fields, there are far more people in musical theater than there are jobs available. To have a good chance at success, you must first be an incredible performer. In most fields, this may simply mean that you need to be good in your primary area. For musical theater performers, the truly successful people are equally skilled in singing, acting, and dancing. There are also a number of newer productions that require the onstage performers to play an instrument of some kind.

You also need to have a good knowledge of the standard repertoire (common songs) for your voice type and be able to memorize a part quickly. Along these lines, you need to be able to perform the roles for which you are typed. This means that your physical build, age, gender, and voice type may determine the parts for which you should audition. You need to know the parts that fit your type and be able to sing the repertoire for that type. Finally, it is helpful if you have a good knowledge of music theory, can read music, can play piano, and have a good ear.

Nonmusical Skills

Performing in musical theater requires a very diverse array of nonmusical skills. First, you need to have a good background in acting and multiple styles of dancing (jazz, tap, ballet, modern, and partner dancing). Next, auditioning for musical theater is more than simply reading an excerpt from a script. Auditioning for this genre usually includes reading a script, singing a short song of your choosing, and learning a short dance. An audition is your chance to reveal the extent of your abilities in a short amount of time. Therefore, you need to know how to audition well.

You also need to know how to analyze a part well. This ability will help you select the best part for your voice type and physical characteristics, and will increase the likelihood that you will win a part. Your ability to analyze a role will also help you learn more about your character and his or her part of the overall production. This type of analysis or preparation is impressive to directors and will likely build your reputation in the industry.

Next, you need to have a good business background. As business skills pertain to musical theater performers, you need to be able to manage your finances and have a thorough knowledge of legal issues pertaining to your contract with the production company to help you maintain steady employment. You should also have some experience in marketing and public relations, and know how to promote yourself as a performer.

Finally, because there are many more performers than there are roles, you need to take extra steps to build a strong reputation for yourself as a performer and as an employee. The skills that will help build this reputation include a strong sense of professionalism, people skills, and communication skills. People skills are especially important in this field as musical theater is such a collaborative art form and every aspect of the success of the production is contingent on your ability to work with people.

Musical Interests

Most musical theater performers express a general interest in singing and dancing. It is also helpful if you love the genre of musical theater and the combination of all the different elements involved with producing a musical theater performance. Most musical theater professionals state that they entered the career field because of favorable experiences in high school performing ensembles or stage acting.

Nonmusical Interests

In addition to the musical interests listed previously, most musical theater performers express an interest in acting. Also, musical theater performers attest that there is a very strong camaraderie that forms among cast members in the process of preparing for productions. This camaraderie also extends into the costume designers, set designers, and other backstage workers who contribute to the production. These friendships, in combination with the lights and glamour of stage performing, create a unique atmosphere that draws musical theater performers to this field.

Musical Work Values (How You Feel Musically Rewarded)

Musical theater performers state that they feel most rewarded by the ability to perform the music that they love, by performing a wide variety of music, and by becoming a part of the musical theater tradition. They also feel rewarded by bringing a part to life, or becoming the character, and the excitement that this brings to the live performance.

Nonmusical Work Values (How You Feel Personally or Professionally Rewarded)

Musical theater professionals feel rewarded by the impact that their performances have on audience members and by the bonds that are created with fellow performers through the production. They enjoy communicating with the audience through their parts, the ability to express themselves through a part, and growing as performers.

Personal Characteristics

The most crucial trait of musical theater performers, particularly those in the early stages of their careers, is an ability and willingness to make an honest self-assessment of their skills, weaknesses, and specifically of their physical build and voice type. According to musical theater professionals, there are several distinct voice types, body builds, and other characteristics that determine the parts for which a person should audition. Musicians who have assessed their abilities as performers will be more fully aware of their strengths, weaknesses, musical abilities, and other characteristics, and of the parts that fit their types. These musicians may therefore experience more success in auditions.

There are also some musical theater performers who possess an extra, indescribable performance trait in addition to the musical and nonmusical skills required of the career field. This attribute has been unofficially labeled in the profession as the "it" factor. Some musical theater professionals suggest that the "it" factor is an indescribable quality that emanates from a performer. Others describe this factor as a presence or charisma that radiates into the audience. Others still suggest that the "it" factor is hard to describe, easy to identify when observed in a performer, and impossible to teach. You either have it or you don't.

When discussing the "it" factor, musical theater performers commonly include a brief discussion of the honest self-assessment trait that was previously discussed. Specifically, musical theater professionals suggest that performers should be keenly aware of their own abilities and should be able to recognize whether or not they possess the "it" factor. Musical theater performers who recognize that they do not possess this attribute may initially feel that they will not be successful as performers. On the contrary, performers without this characteristic may find success but may have to work harder than performers with a higher degree of natural ability.

In addition to these traits, you need to have a very strong work ethic, especially as you work to enter the career field. You need to have confidence, self-discipline, and intelligence. You need to be a good colleague, willing to prepare your part, and an ability to work with a diverse group of coworkers. Finally, musical theater directors are not reputed for being easy on performers. Therefore, you need to be resilient, possess an ability to accept criticism, and be able to deal with disappointment.

THIRTEEN

Bachelor of Music in Music Business/Industry

A degree in music business opens the doors to perhaps the most diverse of all music career fields. If any sort of generalization or categorization could be made, a degree in music business prepares you for one of two main areas. The first area of music business is the popular music industry. Professionals in this field spend most of their time surrounded by popular musicians and the glitz, glamour, and lifestyle of the popular music culture. To describe this aspect of music business concisely, one could say that the primary professional responsibilities are to help performers sound good, get jobs, and help their dreams of stardom come true.

Second, although the term *music business* is more commonly associated with the popular music industry, the term also applies to art music. Specifically, most major symphony orchestras, opera companies, ballet companies, musical theater companies, and other performing arts organizations hire a team of administrators, or music business professionals, who work behind the scenes to organize performers and productions. In this aspect of music business, the professional duties are similar to those described for the popular music industry, but with a focus on symphonies, operas, ballets, and related performance venues.

Because there is such a diverse range of job opportunities, there is an equally diverse range of skills and interests for career compatibility, and locations where a person interested in the music industry may want to live. In addition, university music business programs vary quite a bit from one college to another, based on the university's location or curricular focus. Students who are interested in pursuing a career in the music industry should research the music business programs at a variety of universities and apply to the colleges whose programs address specific career goals and interests.

Some professionals in the music industry may tell you that certain parts of the job market are shrinking. For example, ten years ago, when a popular musician made a new CD, the record label hired graphic artists to design the CD cover and image for the performer, sound engineers to record the music, a person to copy the sound recording from the CD master to the copies for distribution, and warehouse personnel to package the CDs and send them to the stores.

Currently, however, most new songs are recorded digitally and go straight from the soundboard to a website where consumers purchase digital recordings of individual songs or download entire song lists to digital listening devices. Therefore, record labels no longer need to hire so many people to produce and market a CD.

Conversely, other professionals in the music industry suggest that the field is constantly growing. Specifically, musicians have begun to realize that they may not need to go through large record labels such as Warner Bros., Sony, or BMI to get their music distributed to the public. Many new groups, now called indie (short for independent) musicians, are either doing all their own work or are hiring smaller companies and individuals to market their music and post recordings to the band's website.

People on both sides of the argument agree, however, that the music industry is a constantly changing field, perhaps due to technology, or perhaps due to the rapidly changing tastes of music consumers. Whatever the reason, the music industry today may look nothing like the music industry five years from now.

CAREER ENTRY

There are two schools of thought in the music industry concerning the best way to enter this career field. There are many professionals in the music industry who do not have a college degree. In some cases, these people knew somebody on the inside track and were hired because they knew the right people.

Although knowing somebody may get you a good job in the music industry, you will not be able to keep the job unless you have the right skills. To address skills, the opposing belief held by some people is that you must have a degree in music business, business, sound engineering/technology, or a related field for career entry in music business. Through the process of obtaining the degree, you learn the skills and job tasks, and meet the people you need to know to be successful in the field.

Career entry may also be possible through internship programs. Larger companies commonly hire interns who work at minimal pay, if any, performing a random assortment of entry-level tasks. Although the tasks may feel demeaning, the point is to learn the trade from the ground up and work your way up the career ladder.

If you choose to pursue an undergraduate degree in music business, most university music business programs include an internship requirement. The internship is typically completed during the last semester of your course work, just before graduation, and may commonly lead to employment in the company in which you interned.

THE JOBS

There are many jobs in the music industry for people who are perhaps interested in music or who enjoy music but may be gifted in other areas. Some may also tell you that most people in entry-level music business positions are aspiring musicians who pursued nonmusical jobs on a temporary basis so that they could enter the industry with the hopes of one day becoming performers. It is up to you to evaluate whether you should pursue a career as a popular musician or other type of performer, or if you are content to run the soundboard, represent performing artists, or fulfill other managerial or administrative roles.

Also, specific job functions and duties change based on the size of the company for which you want to work. In smaller companies, it is common for people to have two or more titles and to do the work of several people. In very large companies, one job title and its related duties may be shared by two or more people. University music business programs can provide you with much more specific details about the types of jobs, the ways that jobs vary based on company size and location, and the specific function of jobs in these companies. Because the jobs in music business are so diverse, they have been categorized into the following four categories: arts administration, record labels, publishing, and other.

Arts Administration

Most administrative jobs require you to be a detail-oriented and task-oriented person. Administrators are typically responsible for making sure other employees are doing their jobs. Usually, administrators started in entry-level positions or as interns and worked their way up the career ladder, usually through several different jobs within the music industry.

Concert Production

Concert producers usually handle all the administrative details of organizing or producing a concert. They may have to reserve a performance facility, see that the stage is set, make sure that the dressing rooms are ready, hire sound technicians, rent the necessary equipment, hire an equipment crew to set everything up, and see that all other details have been addressed.

Marketing

The main duty of people in marketing is to make the public aware of a new CD or new song, or increase the public's awareness of a new product, musical group, or soloist. Marketing specialists work with design teams and graphic artists to create posters, flyers, website pages, and other visual means of promoting their clients. Marketing specialists also promote their clients by developing commercials and promotional audio or video clips to broadcast on local radio and television stations.

Development

Development usually refers to fundraising and is more commonly associated with performing arts organizations rather than the popular music side of the music industry. Musicians in this field usually work for arts organizations, nonprofit organizations, or performance halls whose budget is based primarily on donations and grants.

Concert Promotion

Concert promoters are hired by performance halls or related organizations to make sure the general public knows about upcoming events. Promoters contact local radio stations, newspapers, or trade magazines, or create television commercials publicizing upcoming concerts and events. They may also be responsible for ticket sales, communication with donors, or reserving complimentary tickets and stage passes for friends and family of the performers.

Record Labels

When a new group wants to release a CD, they will need a record label to record, produce, and market their music. Record labels are responsible for these aspects and generally creating the overall image of the group.

Sound Engineer

Sound engineers record music using various recording technologies and must have an extensive knowledge of recording techniques, acoustics, the newest microphones and soundboards, digital recording, and many other aspects of technology. As stated in the introduction of this book, there is a Bachelor of Music in Electrical Engineering/Recording Technology, and a small number of colleges are beginning to offer this degree. There are also a larger number of junior colleges and technical or trade schools that offer associate's degrees in this field. Additional information about this career field can be found in chapter 14 of this book.

Artist and Repertoire (A&R)

Larger companies hire a person whose sole responsibility is to find new songwriters, peruse their songs, and find materials that will hopefully be the new hit. A&R people also act as talent scouts, searching for the next big names in popular music. After finding new talent and musical selections, the A&R person matches the new hit with a singer whose voice and overall image best fits that song. A&R people must have an excellent ear for what sounds good and an ability to predict which songs and entertainers will be the new number-one single on the popular charts.

Record Company Management

Managers are responsible for all the administrative details of a record company. The managers usually hire and fire employees and have the final say in whether the record company will accept a new artist, use a new song, or promote a particular concert tour.

Publishing

The publishing side of the music industry deals with getting the product (printed music, sound recordings, CDs, and other music-related merchandise) from the manufacturers to the consumers. This part of the industry also protects the ownership of the printed and recorded music to ensure that copyright laws are enforced and thereby guarantee that the people who created and recorded the music are paid the appropriate royalties.

Licensing

Whenever a school choir, cover band, or other musician wants to perform a song that is protected by copyright law, the performers must obtain the correct licenses or permissions to perform the music, copy the music for the performers, and/or distribute recordings of the song. For situations such as these, the performer contacts a representative who specializes in licensing.

Licensing personnel work closely with performers and their representatives to negotiate the terms of the proposed performance and agree on certain conditions under which the group may perform, record, or sell the song. Sometimes, publishing companies hire a licensing person to visit local nightclubs and similar venues to ensure that the DJs and per-

formers have obtained the necessary permission to perform or play recordings of songs that are protected by copyright.

Broadcast

People in broadcast typically work in radio stations, either as DJs or
general managers of radio stations or in other administrative roles. Musicians in broadcast careers may announce songs on the radio, interview
artists, report the news, attend premieres of new bands or songs, sell
advertising space for radio stations, and fulfill additional duties.

Entertainment Law

There is a lot of crossover concerning jobs in entertainment law and
copyright law. Musicians in entertainment law usually deal with copyright issues but may also communicate with performers' work unions,
negotiate contracts between performers and their recording companies,
and negotiate fees with talent agents. This aspect of the music industry
also ensures that all other contractual agreements are kept. Many people
in this sector of the music industry have as much training and experience
in law as they do in music.

Copyright and Intellectual Property Rights

Musicians employed in these positions are the experts in copyright
law. The primary duty of these musicians is to ensure that people are not
illegally copying sheet music, downloading bootlegged songs, or in any
other way violating copyright laws related to music.

Distribution

The primary duty in distribution is to get the product to the consumer.
In the music industry, the term *product* may mean anything from CDs,
sheet music, and instruments, to posters, T-shirts or other music-related
memorabilia. Distributors may tour with a performing group to see that
all the souvenir tables at the concerts are stocked with the latest items or
may serve as a liaison between publishing companies and local music or
department stores that carry the company's products.

Other Music Business Careers

Music Products

Publishing companies and record labels commonly hire graphic artists and salespeople to design, produce, market, and sometimes distribute any product that will promote a solo artist or a group and their music.
Some people work for a single company, while others may work on a

per-contract basis, making and selling music products for a number of different organizations. In some cases, instrument manufacturing companies hire people to market their instruments to local music stores and college or high school music programs.

Composing

Although composition has its own career field and related degree, there are many composers who work directly with the music industry rather than with symphony orchestras or opera houses. Typically, composition in the music industry is specific to music for websites, video games, commercial jingles, television shows, and movie sound tracks.

Music Supervisors

The job of a music supervisor is to work with a television or movie director and producer to select or arrange music for a movie or television program, based on the director's vision and the show's theme. Once the music supervisor has an idea of the type of sound the director has in mind, he or she researches certain types of music to give the director the desired sound. Supervisors also work as liaisons between directors and composers to help composers create the most appropriate music.

Booking/Tour Management

A booker or tour manager works directly with performers and record companies to arrange concert tours. The tour manager reserves performance facilities, makes travel arrangements, and works with marketers, music product specialists, and other people who organize other aspects of the tour. The tour manager may also hire and fire sound engineers, road crew, and the other personnel needed for a performing tour, and ensure that all the required equipment has been arranged.

Teaching Music Business Courses at the College Level

In order for the music business to survive, the industry must have teachers to prepare the next generation of professionals. Music business teachers are usually people who have spent a few years in the industry and desire to pass their skills and experience along to a new generation of musicians by teaching at the college level. There are also a select number of magnet or performing arts high schools that may hire a music business teacher to enhance their programs.

MOST PROMISING LOCATIONS

The most promising locations in the music industry depend on the type of job you want to pursue. In most cases, it is helpful if you live near or in a large city with multiple concert halls, performance facilities, and recording studios. Specifically, cities like Nashville and Los Angeles are good locations for studio work, particularly in country and popular music, respectively. Los Angeles is also a very active city for studio musicians who record movie and television soundtracks. You may also find a lot of work in concert promotion in cities like New York or Chicago that have a lot of performance venues.

WHAT DOES IT TAKE TO BE A GOOD FIT IN THE MUSIC INDUSTRY?

Musical Skills

You need to have a keen understanding of what sounds good, particularly if you plan to work in the recording business. You must also know the current popular music market and be able to either predict future trends or react to trends quickly to be successful. Although you may not need to be a masterful singer or performer on an instrument, it is helpful if you are proficient on at least one instrument and as a singer so that you can relate to the performers and help them be successful. Similarly, you should have a working knowledge of music theory and music history. Knowledge in these areas may help you improve the quality of the music and ensure that it has been performed in the appropriate musical style when necessary.

Nonmusical Skills

Because there are so many business-related aspects of most jobs in the music industry, you should have skills and training in finance and accounting. You should have a general understanding of business, copyright and intellectual property rights, and marketing. Finally, as so many jobs deal with sound or recording technology, you should be skilled in these areas as well.

Musical Interests

Typically, music business deals with popular music genres. As a result, you should have a strong interest in popular or commercial music and a desire to be involved in the industry. More clearly, although you may specialize in a particular genre of popular music, you should have a somewhat eclectic listening palate, meaning that it is helpful if you are interested in a wide range of popular musical styles.

The same concept may also be applied to the art music side of the music industry. If you want to work as an administrator for a symphony, opera company, or related business, you need to have an eclectic listening palate as it pertains to art music. You should also be aware that other types of ensembles and touring musicians commonly perform in large auditoriums and concert halls, so it is helpful if your listening and musical awareness extends into other genres.

Nonmusical Interests

Very few of the jobs in the music industry can be described as typical nine-to-five jobs. You may spend a lot of nights and weekends traveling, attending or producing concerts, touring, or fulfilling other duties that do not always adhere to a typical work schedule. Therefore, to be a good fit you should have a general interest in a nonconventional career. You should also have an interest in the behind-the-scenes aspects of popular music.

Musical Work Values (How You Feel Musically Rewarded)

People in the music industry often have jobs that nobody knows about. It may be best described that your job is to make somebody else sound good and eventually help them become famous. Therefore, it is helpful if you are the type of person who feels rewarded by the ability to be in close proximity to popular musicians and by the ability to be involved in the creative processes of recording and performing. Occasionally, an artist or song to which you contribute may make its way to the top 10. When this happens, you may also feel rewarded by the accolades and praises that come your way.

Nonmusical Work Values (How You Feel Personally or Professionally Rewarded)

Although you may never perform or see your name in lights, you may be a good fit if you feel professionally rewarded by the ability to stay involved with music. You may also feel rewarded by seeing a song or other product transition from its beginning phases all the way through to completion. Finally, music business professionals feel fulfilled by the ability to help performers realize their dreams.

Personal Characteristics

To be a good fit in the music industry, you must have a great deal of drive, perseverance, and tenacity. You must also have a very strong work ethic as the hours can be long and hard. You must have good communication skills, both in writing and verbally. You should be well organized and detail oriented. Due to the importance of marketing and promotion in many music business careers, you should be entrepreneurial and willing to take risks.

You should also have a strong sense of professionalism and the ability to keep your cool when working with famous musicians. You should have an outgoing personality, be thick skinned, and be able to deal with rejection. Finally, the music business is an ever-developing career field. Therefore, you need to be able to adjust to a constantly changing work environment.

FOURTEEN

Bachelor of Music in Electrical Engineering/Recording Technology

Sound engineers are needed anywhere there are live performances, public presentations, or recording studios. Generally speaking, sound engineers set up and run sound amplification systems and recording equipment in concert halls, public arenas, churches, and recording studios. Sometimes, sound engineers design and manufacture public address (PA) systems, speakers, microphones, or the materials used by architects and construction firms to manipulate the acoustic properties of public performance halls.

Like all music careers that use technology, the job description of sound engineers has drastically evolved in recent years to encompass many new hardware and software applications for sound engineering. In just a few years, bulky equipment that required hours of setup and endless spools of cable has been replaced by sleek, handheld devices that function wirelessly and fit on performers' stands or instruments. There are also many free, downloadable apps that enable just about anyone to record his or her own music with some degree of proficiency. As a result, this is an ever-changing career field, providing for an extensive range of career opportunities.

CAREER ENTRY

There are many jobs in this career field that are available to musicians who do not hold a college degree. As of this writing, there are fewer than five universities in the United States that offer a Bachelor of Music degree in sound engineering and recording technology. A significantly larger number of universities offers a bachelor's degree in sound engineering through mass communications departments or through radio and television broadcast programs.

It is much more common, however, to find technical colleges and community colleges that offer associates degrees in sound engineering or electrical engineering with an emphasis in recording technology. In some programs, you may also receive a certificate or electrician's license in addition to or in lieu of a formal degree.

In either case, these two-year programs usually provide adequate training and experience for most careers in sound engineering and recording technology. Some jobs in larger industries, performing venues, or universities may require a four-year degree, or a graduate degree may be required to teach sound engineering at the college level.

THE JOBS

The most common job in this field is to work as a sound engineer for recording studios or live performances. Sound engineers are hired by large performance venues such as concert halls, arenas, auditoriums, and convention centers. Some businesses, corporations, or campuses also hire sound engineers to manage equipment and run sound systems for larger meeting rooms and performance halls. Sound engineers are also hired by theme parks, cruise ships, and hotels that frequently host musical events or social gatherings.

In larger cities, there may be churches and other religious congregations that hire full-time sound engineers, although it is much more common to find part-time or volunteer sound engineers in churches. Touring performers, bands, and other ensembles may also hire sound engineers to set up, manage, and run sound for live concerts. Finally, sound engineers are employed by television, movie, and recording studios, particularly in larger cities across the country.

There is a lot of freelance work in sound engineering that commonly crosses over into other types of careers. Sometimes, sound engineers are also independent musicians or band members, and manage their own sound equipment for recording and live performances. There is also a lot of crossover into other multimedia or audio-video performance venues — specifically, music and video production, music and light or laser shows, and music and pyrotechnics (fireworks).

Both in live performance and in recording studios, there is a lot of crossover into other forms of movie, television, or radio production. For example, a music DJ with extensive experience in mixing may also be responsible for managing other types of recording equipment. Sound engineers may also be required to set up stage lights or choreograph the lights to the music or other aspects of the performance.

There are a lot of crossover careers in sound engineering and architecture or construction. Sound engineers are sometimes hired by construction companies or architectural firms to design sound systems for concert halls, performance halls, rehearsal spaces, or recording spaces. Sound engineers may also be hired to design and/or install other aspects of large performing venues including sound shells, choir risers, acoustic paneling or curtains, and practice spaces.

Finally, there is a significant number of sound engineering careers in sales and promotion. Manufacturers of sound systems, hardware, and software companies commonly hire people with training and experience in sound engineering to promote and sell their products. These companies may also hire sound engineers to design and manufacture new products, or conduct research that may eventually result in a new product.

MOST PROMISING LOCATIONS

As with most other music careers, the most promising location depends on the type of career you want to have. If you plan to work in recording studios, you may need to consider moving to Nashville, New York, Los Angeles, or other large cities with a significant number of recording studios. Most urban areas will have multiple performing venues for live musicians where sound engineers may be employed. In suburban and rural areas, it may be difficult to find full-time employment in sound engineering, unless you run sound systems for a corporation or work in sales.

WHAT DOES IT TAKE TO BE A GOOD FIT IN ELECTRICAL ENGINEERING/RECORDING TECHNOLOGY?

Musical Skills

First and foremost, you must have an excellent ear. More specifically, you must be able to hear very subtle differences in tone, texture, and other nuisances of a sound, and use technology to manipulate the sound until it meets the desired expectation. To achieve this goal, it is helpful if you have a thorough knowledge of music acoustics and properties of sound (amplitude, frequency, etc.), and how music technology relates to these properties.

It is also helpful if you have some fundamental competency as a performer, either as an instrumentalist or as a vocalist, so you will know how to meet a performer's expectations. It may be more desirable to learn the basics of an instrument that is more reliant on sound systems (electric guitar or bass) than an acoustic instrument (trumpet or violin) as you will be more likely to learn more about sound engineering through your own performance. This experience will also help you learn how to listen for instrumental tone, ensemble balance, and musical texture, and to manipulate sound technology to produce the best overall sound.

Lastly, you must have a thorough knowledge of the type of music most closely related to your career goals. If you plan to mix, DJ, or provide entertainment music for social gatherings, you must know the most relevant and current music for your audiences. Or, if you plan to run sound system for a performing ensemble, you must know the group's music well enough to know when to activate and deactivate certain microphones or other devices.

Nonmusical Skills

Because electrical engineers deal extensively with recording hardware and software, it is essential that you have an extensive knowledge of the terms, tools, and concepts affiliated with the related technology. In addition, you need to know how to apply these terms and concepts to the technology in a variety of contexts.

It is also essential that you possess a thorough knowledge of the properties of sound (acoustic physics) and know how to manipulate various aspects of sound through technology and the use of space. This requires both musical skill and nonmusical skill as it addresses pitch, dynamics, and tone as much as it addresses frequency, amplitude, and other sound wave characteristics more commonly associated with acoustic physics than music.

Next, you must have a bent toward technology as hardware and software are the primary means of amplifying, mixing, and recording sound. You must also have the ability and willingness to remain current on the most recent hardware and software applications for sound engineering.

Business skills are also essential, particularly for sound engineers in the earliest phases of their careers or who serve multiple functions. For example, if you wish to perform as an independent musician and run your own sound system, business skills are essential to market and promote your band, manage your band's finances, and handle other managerial responsibilities. Also, in some recording studios, the sound engineer may be asked to manage inventory and budgets for purchasing new equipment, hire additional sound engineers, and estimate costs for recording sessions.

You must also be able to solve problems very quickly, usually through a keen attention to detail pertaining to sound. When feedback occurs, for example, you must be able to immediately identify the source of the feedback and fix the problem without undue attention to the error. As another common example, an electrical short in a cable, a broken fuse, or dead battery may cause costly delays to the start of a large event. It is usually the responsibility of the sound engineer to identify the cause of the problem and remedy the situation so the event can start in a timely manner.

Next, you must possess the ability and willingness to repeatedly complete tedious tasks. A sound engineer for a touring group or solo performer, for example, is responsible for setting up a sound system before every performance, running the system during the concert, tearing down equipment after the show, and managing equipment between concerts. In a busy touring season, this process may be repeated five to fifteen times each week and can easily become repetitious.

It should also be noted that this ability to repeat tedious tasks multiple times should coincide with the attention to detail that was already discussed. It may be easy to become sloppy or careless in tedious tasks, but with sound systems, careless work leads to poorly functioning or malfunctioning equipment, and can easily ruin or end a sound engineer's career.

Finally, as a sound engineer, you should possess enough physical strength to fulfill the tasks of your job. A sound engineer in a studio may deal primarily with smaller equipment, so the physical demands are not too strenuous. A sound engineer for a touring musician, however, may be required to lift incredibly large speakers, monitors, soundboards, or other equipment, and physical stamina and strength are essential for the job.

Musical Interests

Sound engineers are usually interested in being surrounded by live music, either in front of audiences or in a recording studio, and in the process of making a live concert event come together. In this aspect, sound engineers design specific sound system configurations for different events or performance venues, set up and test the equipment before the event, and run the equipment during the performance. This process feeds their interests in sound systems and related technology and in live music performance. Many sound engineers are also part-time performers and therefore have an interest in instrumental or vocal performance. Sound engineers also commonly state that they are interested in being surrounded by performers and by the excitement of live musical events but prefer to stay behind the scenes and avoid the stress and unpredictability of live performance.

Nonmusical Interests

Sound engineering requires extensive knowledge and aptitude for technology. Therefore, sound engineers are commonly interested in computers, hardware, software, digital media, and other technological advances in music, and manipulating sound through digital and electronic means. Sound engineers are also commonly interested in wiring and electrical engineering as this is a major component of the job description.

Next, managing a sound system and running a system effectively requires a thorough knowledge of sound, the properties of sound, and acoustic physics. Therefore, many sound engineers state that their love of music is matched with an interest in science, with a particular focus on the physics of sound.

Many sound engineers also manage some of the business-related aspects of their careers, so a general interest in business is recommended. In these instances, the term *business* may apply to marketing yourself as a sound engineer, DJ, or performer managing the finances for a recording studio or performance hall, or any number of additional business-related functions.

Finally, sound engineers are required to tailor a sound system to match the size, dimensions, and other characteristics of a particular building. As such, sound engineers are usually interested in, and moderately knowledgeable about, architecture, and they use this knowledge to obtain the best possible sound in a given performance or recording space.

Musical Work Values (How You Feel Musically Rewarded)

Sound engineers commonly say that they feel rewarded by making an ensemble or solo performer sound good and by helping the live performer fulfill his or her dreams. They feel rewarded by the hard work it takes to set up for a performance and seeing all the pieces come together for the event. Lastly, they feel rewarded by the ability to support themselves doing what they love and the ability to stay involved in live and recorded music.

Nonmusical Work Values (How You Feel Personally or Professionally Rewarded)

Sound engineers feel nonmusically rewarded by the ability to use their creativity to solve the multiple, unpredictable problems that are a natural part of technology. Mostly, they enjoy the diagnosis/prognosis process of finding a problem, solving it quickly, and enabling the musicians to continue performing or recording.

Sound engineers also feel rewarded by contributing to the success of a musical event. Specifically, they feel rewarded by helping the performers feel successful and helping audience members enjoy a live musical event. In the case of recorded music, they enjoy seeing and listening to the finished package (the CD or audio download) and knowing that they played a small part in the completion of that project.

Personal Characteristics

Sound engineers work with all types of people and must possess the people skills necessary to professionally interact with musicians, technicians, producers, directors, agents, and a multitude of other colleagues. As a sound engineer, you must also have a great deal of patience as there are many tedious tasks involved in managing sound equipment, particularly in recording studios. Patience will enable you to maintain focus through a twelve-hour recording session, keep your cool when the sound system continually malfunctions, and generally, perform the professional functions required of you.

You must also possess a great deal of tenacity that is matched with an equal amount of meticulousness. The slightest turn of a button or movement of a slider on a soundboard can have a significant effect on the quality of a sound. Likewise, in several thousand feet of electrical wiring, there may be one bad plug or wire that needs to be replaced. It will take extreme attention to detail and persistence to fulfill these types of professional responsibilities that are common for sound engineers.

Next you must be able to multitask. Sound engineers usually have very busy schedules and have several projects in various stages of development. As an example, you may be in the recording stage of one project while editing another and simultaneously interviewing support staff or studio musicians for an upcoming performance or recording session. Therefore, multitasking is an essential trait for sound engineers.

You must also be flexible and willing to put other people's agendas ahead of your own. A performer, for example, may want you to make him or her sound a certain way on a recording even when you feel he or she should sound differently. A producer may want a certain mix when you feel the music would sound better with a different balance. This flexibility must also be matched with diplomacy, or an ability to make suggestions for improvement without hurting fragile egos or overstepping your boundaries.

Finally, you must be content to work behind the scenes for extended periods of time with little or no recognition. This ability must be matched with a very thick skin and a very cool temper. Rarely do sound engineers receive accolades for the success of a record or live performance. However, when some aspect of a sound system malfunctions, there is considerable potential for the sound engineer to receive undue complaints, glares, and criticism. You must be willing and able to work in this kind of environment, where there may be little public recognition for your efforts.

FIFTEEN

Bachelor of Music in Music Therapy

Although the use of music in therapeutic settings has been in practice for a number of years, music therapy as formal study is one of the newer music career fields. It is also one of the most standardized career fields because all music therapy training programs and practicing professionals are required to receive accreditation from the same organization (American Music Therapy Association [AMTA]). The implementation of nationally adopted accreditation standards has generated considerable stability in music therapy as compared to education, for example, where each state sets its own standards for teacher certification.

Some music therapists compare this career field to that of music education, specifically when teaching music to children with special needs. Other music therapists suggest that there are stark differences between music education and music therapy as the point of music therapy is not necessarily to teach people about music, but to use music to heal some sort of physical handicap, mental or emotional illness, behavioral disorder, or other condition.

Because music therapy is comparatively new, there are many who do not fully understand the purpose of this career field. As a result, you may notice music therapy grouped among many other career fields in music career texts and online resources. Because of the unique nature of music therapy, and because a specific degree is required for career entry, it is most appropriate to avoid grouping music therapy with other music career fields.

CAREER ENTRY

During the interviews with musicians for this book, music therapy was the only music career field in which participants noted that the degree was required for all careers in the field. Furthermore, a music therapist is not fully qualified without also obtaining the national music therapy certification from the AMTA. The AMTA has published set of nationally implemented competencies that must be met by all music therapists graduating from an AMTA-accredited music therapy program. These competencies have provided very clear guidelines concerning the musical and nonmusical expectations for current and future music therapists.

THE JOBS

As is stated in the general description, there is a great deal of confusion, even among professional musicians, about what a music therapist is and what a music therapist actually does. Simply stated, a music therapist may be described as any other type of therapist whose goal is to improve a particular aspect of another person's quality of life. Obviously, a music therapist uses music as a tool to that end.

In most music career fields, there are a variety of careers from which to choose. In music therapy, however, the point of entering the career field is to become a music therapist. Therefore, there may initially seem to be considerably fewer career options in music therapy. In addition to becoming a licensed therapist, you may become an administrator of a music therapy program or teach in a university music therapy training program.

Although there may seem to be fewer career options, therapists suggest an incredible diversity concerning the types of people and disabilities with whom music therapists work, and professional locations where music therapists may be employed. Music therapists are commonly employed by hospitals, independent clinics, school systems, community-based programs, nursing homes or hospice care, extended care facilities, treatment centers, rehabilitation centers, psychiatric wards, brain injury centers, and prisons.

As for clientele, music therapists work in neonatal facilities with babies in utero, senior citizens in hospice care, and any age in between. Regarding disabilities, music therapists may specialize in physical handicaps or rehabilitation, developmental delays, behavioral disorders, emotional disorders, or behavioral issues. Again, the primary goal of music therapists is to use music as a tool to cure any number of diagnosed conditions with which their clients struggle.

MOST PROMISING LOCATIONS

There may be some medical centers, rehabilitation facilities, or other locations that do not hire music therapists simply because they are unaware of music therapy. However, most of the larger, more up-to-date facilities maintain active research agendas in best practices and are therefore aware of this growing career field. Consequently, jobs are available in most cities that have medium to large resources in any of the areas previously listed.

WHAT DOES IT TAKE TO BE A GOOD FIT IN MUSIC THERAPY?

Musical Skills

According to the music therapists who were interviewed for this book, the AMTA publishes a list of nationally adopted competencies for music therapy. Most of the musical and nonmusical skills included in this book were excerpted from the published list. Because all university music therapy programs are held to these standards, any accredited program should offer similar training to prepare you for the national board certification exam and for the career field.

First, you need to be proficient on the piano, guitar, and a variety of percussion instruments, and as a singer. You need to be able to improvise well, have a general knowledge of music acoustics, be comfortable with movement and dance, know how to transpose songs into various keys to match the voices of your clients, and have a general knowledge of other music instruments.

Nonmusical Skills

Because the point of music therapy is to interact with people, you need to have excellent interpersonal skills and communication skills, specifically with people who possess a variety of special needs. Also in this role, it is helpful if you have some experience with psychology and behavior management. You also need to be able to help people integrate music with their personal lives.

As a music therapist, you need to have good research and writing skills. Specifically, you may need to research the disabilities and disorders of your clients to prescribe the best course of treatment. You also need to be able to diagnose or assess your clients and prescribe the most likely process of treatment. In this role, you may also need to write diagnoses, letters describing a course of treatment, or any number of other formal documents.

Finally, as a music therapist you may be expected to juggle a number of tasks at any given time. Therefore, you need to be able to multitask. You will also face a variety of unexpected circumstances in your job. To deal professionally with unexpected events or situations, you must have an ability to think on your feet.

Musical Interests

Many music therapists may have been drawn to the music therapy career field because they witnessed a close friend or family member suffer some type of physical or emotional trauma. Others may have acquaintances with a physical or mental handicap, neurological or developmental delay, or other type of disability. Others still may have struggled through their own emotional or psychological issues, and want to help other people with similar difficulties.

Although situations such as these may instill an interest in working with special populations, music therapists must be emotionally stable and possess a certain degree of emotional stamina rather than having to deal with their own emotional issues in addition to those of their clients. Generally, music therapists need to have a strong desire to help people through music, a general interest in music, and a desire to stay involved in music.

Nonmusical Interests

Although music therapists are trained to deal with a variety of people and disabilities, most specialize in a particular area or age group. Therefore, you need to have a desire to work with a specific population or disability. It is also helpful if you are interested in psychology, medicine, working in a service organization of some kind, and in developing one-on-one professional relationships with clients.

Musical Work Values (How You Feel Musically Rewarded)

Music therapists feel most rewarded when they are able to use music to improve somebody else's quality of life. They are most rewarded when people with no prior musical experiences are able to participate in some way with music. They also value the spontaneous nature of music, using music to connect with other people, and the ability to stay involved with music throughout their careers.

Nonmusical Work Values (How You Feel Personally or Professionally Rewarded)

Similar to the musical work values listed, music therapists feel rewarded by helping people succeed, mature, and change over time. They value forming relationships with their clients and generating a professional network with other musicians. Finally, music therapists feel rewarded by professional variety, the ability to contribute to the body of research and knowledge in the field, and connecting music with other aspects of life.

Personal Characteristics

The two personal characteristics that are the most essential traits for music therapists are emotional stability and maturity. Music therapists work in potentially sensitive environments and with clients of varying disabilities. Because continued exposure to these environments may quickly become emotionally taxing, emotional stability and maturity are necessary traits for music therapists who spend extended periods of time in challenging situations.

Music therapists also need to be compassionate and patient as they work with clients, helping them overcome their issues and manage their disabilities. Music therapists also need to be respectful because a primary component of their jobs is dealing with sensitive circumstances and vulnerable populations. It is also helpful in this environment that they have a good sense of humor.

Because music therapy is such a people-oriented career field, it is helpful if you are outgoing and confident. You also need to be flexible and spontaneous to deal with the unanticipated events or circumstances that may occur during a music therapy session. You also need to be selfless, willing to give of yourself and of your time to people who may not be able to reciprocate your generosity. Finally, in a career with very high professional expectations, you need to be motivated, dependable, and detail oriented.

SIXTEEN

Bachelor of Music in Music Education

Music education is one of the most well-known music career fields and offers a wide array of professional opportunities. Although teaching can be a challenging field, music educators feel that it can be one of the most rewarding careers as a musician. Music educators sometimes suggest that music education provides the foundation for musical success in all other music career fields. Therefore, without music educators there would be no performers, music therapists, music business professionals, theorists, composers, or other musicians.

CAREER ENTRY

Becoming a music teacher is most commonly accomplished by completing a university music teacher preparation program and obtaining a teaching license from your state of residence. Because music teacher education programs lead to a state-sponsored teacher certification, specific requirements may vary from state to state, but there is a general consensus concerning requirements for teacher licensure.

Many states also offer some form of alternative certification indicating that musicians can become teachers without obtaining an undergraduate degree in music education. To be clear, you do need an undergraduate degree for alternative licensure, but that degree does not need to be in music.

As a caveat, alternative certification programs were originally designed for people who have spent a number of years in a career field and wish to become teachers, but who may not have the time or resources to quit work long enough to go back to college for an additional degree. In music, for example, a seasoned symphony musician with twenty years of experience in performance may want to become a high school orchestra director. This musician may be hired with a temporary teacher license and under a cooperative agreement that he or she will take weekend or evening courses in an alternative-certification program to receive a teaching license while working for the school.

Over time, a misunderstanding of the intent of alternative certification has led many students to pursue this certification rather than completing a traditional music education program. For instance, students who may not be able to pass a course in the music education degree plan may pursue a different music degree that does not require the music education course and pursue alternative certification after college.

As another scenario, most music degrees can be completed in four years. A music education degree, however, typically requires additional courses including a semester or more of student teaching. Music students who may want to become music educators but also want to graduate in four years sometimes pursue other music degrees and seek alternative certification after graduation.

You should be aware that alternative certification programs are generally viewed unfavorably by school administrators, and it may be difficult to obtain employment with an alternative certification. Furthermore, research indicates that most alternatively certified educators either quit or are fired within three years because they are not properly trained as educators and are typically less effective than traditionally certified teachers.

If you want to become a music educator, take the extra semester or two to complete a traditional music education degree and certification. You will be much more prepared for your career, and the chances of your success are significantly greater than if you pursue the career through alternative means. One last word on this subject: although alternative certification may seem like a quicker or cheaper route, it can wind up costing you more time and money than if you had obtained a music education degree and teaching license through traditional means. Alternative licensure programs can be very costly and time consuming, and your salary may be about half that of a licensed teacher until you complete your licensure program.

On a different note, many students enter music teacher preparation programs with very clearly defined goals of becoming ensemble directors or elementary music teachers. In their teacher preparation courses, however, they are exposed to other types of music teaching and sometimes discover they are more suited for teaching in an area that they did not originally intend.

Furthermore, most states offer an all-level license for music education. As a result, even though you may intend to teach only high school students, you will be certified to teach all grade levels. Therefore, you will have to take classes that prepare you for elementary through high school music even though you may intend to teach at a particular level. Similarly, students who plan to teach elementary music take instrumental and choral methods courses that enable them to direct secondary ensembles if they so choose.

In these elementary and secondary music methods classes, and in student teaching, students commonly discover that, while they originally intended to teach a specific grade level, they are equally interested and skilled in teaching other ages. Although it is good to have well-defined goals, you should also feel encouraged to keep your options open.

THE JOBS

Although the initial careers in music education may seem obvious, there are also a number of additional careers that may be less common. Typically, music educators specialize in one of the following areas:

- General music for early childhood (infants to preschool)
- General music for elementary school
- Choir director
- Band director
- Orchestra director

Based on the size and administration of the school in which you want to work, there are a number of variations of each of these jobs. In larger school systems, you may work only with beginning ensembles. In smaller schools, you may work multiple grade levels but specialize in one type of instrument (high brass, for example).

There are also a variety of other ensembles for which music teachers may be hired, again depending on the size and location of the school. Some schools are large enough to hire a band director whose sole focus is to direct the jazz ensembles. Mariachi ensembles are also growing in popularity across the United States, particularly in southern states.

In some schools, ensemble directors are also required to teach some type of music appreciation, general music, or introductory music theory courses. There are also instances of very small schools that may hire one music educator who is responsible for all ensembles and music classes for kindergarten through twelfth grade.

Music educators may choose to teach in public, parochial, private, or church-affiliated schools. Most of these careers are also available in schools around the world for children of military personnel who have been stationed overseas. Music educators who wish to pursue graduate degrees may also teach at the college level in music teacher education programs. Music educators may also pursue administrative certifications and become music supervisors, administrators, or associate superintendents who specialize in fine arts administration for school districts.

Larger churches may also employ a children's music specialist who directs children's choirs, hand bell ensembles, and a variety of other children's music programs. Some musicians with music education backgrounds also teach private lessons for schools, for music stores, or independently. There are also a number of community-based programs that offer private or group music lessons and employ musicians with music education backgrounds. Finally, music educators are also employed by local, state, and national music educator or music advocacy organizations.

MOST PROMISING LOCATIONS

Like many other careers, the most promising locations depend on the type of job you want. In larger school systems, you may be hired to teach only one instrument or ensemble, but you will be able to work with students of all ability levels. In other districts you may work with all instruments or voice types but may specialize in one grade, age, or ability level.

Typically, schools in larger districts or with a more diverse student population have a wider array of ensembles and educational opportunities. Rural schools traditionally have smaller budgets, may hire fewer music educators, and have smaller facilities. Overall, it is common for music educators to pursue careers in schools whose size and demographics mirror those of their own educational background and experiences.

WHAT DOES IT TAKE TO BE A GOOD FIT IN MUSIC EDUCATION?

Musical Skills

First and foremost, it is impractical to expect from your students that which you cannot deliver. In the specific context of music education, you cannot expect your students to become strong musicians if you cannot model musicianship for them. Therefore, you must be a strong musician for success as a music educator.

Remember that there is a difference between musician and performer, as is discussed earlier in this book. Do not think you have to be a Broadway or Metropolitan Opera–level performer to be successful as a music educator, but keep in mind that musicianship is a must. Along these lines, you should be knowledgeable in music history and theory, and be able to sight-read and sight-sing.

Also, as a music teacher or ensemble director, you will spend a greater portion of your day helping young musicians improve in their own musical ability. In this role, you will need to be able to identify poor tone, faulty intonation, incorrect fingerings, inaccurate rhythms, balance issues, and a host of other problems. To do this, you must have good aural skills and excellent error detection skills. Also, whether you teach at the elementary or secondary level, you need to be a good conductor.

You must also be very knowledgeable in the related literature for your field. Band directors must know the band literature; elementary music educators must know the folk, traditional, and children's song literature; choir directors must know choral literature; and orchestra directors must know symphonic literature. You must also know the pedagogy, or how to teach the music, of your area of specialization.

It is also helpful if you are competent in a secondary performance area. Instrumental ensemble directors should know the basics of every instrument in their ensembles to teach their students effectively. It is also common for instrumental ensemble directors to sing rhythms and melodies as they help young musicians learn to perform their individual parts. Therefore, it is helpful if you know how to sing.

Similarly, choir directors should be able to sing all parts on a choral score and should be proficient at the keyboard and guitar. Choir directors may also be expected to conduct oratorios, operas, musicals, or other productions where vocalists are accompanied by an instrumental ensemble. To meet this expectation, it is helpful if vocalists have received at least a rudimentary training in instrumental performance and pedagogy.

Nonmusical Skills

First, you must be good with people. Specifically, each age, grade level, and ensemble presents its own unique blend of quirks and oddities. You need to be able to relate well to the age and general demographics of the students you intend to teach. You also need to know the developmental psychology of the students to understand why they can or cannot accomplish certain tasks at certain ages.

You must also be able to manage the behaviors of the students in your care. You must be a strong communicator and be able to present a complicated subject matter in a way that students can comprehend and apply. Finally, because music teachers commonly have a number of different tasks to complete at any given time, you must be a well-organized person.

Musical Interests

Most music educators are led to pursue careers in music education because of their own experiences as music students, particularly in high school performing ensembles. Essentially, music educators chose to enter this career field because they enjoyed performing in high school band, choir, and orchestra, and were inspired by their music teachers to pursue careers in music education. This indicates that music education is a very cyclical field: effective teaching begets effective teaching. If you are considering a career in music education, know that you may one day become the reason that another student chooses to (or not to) become a music educator.

Nonmusical Interests

Because the purpose of music education is to help other people become musical, you need to have an interest in sharing your knowledge and skills with other people and a general desire to work with a particular age group or ensemble.

Musical Work Values (How You Feel Musically Rewarded)

Music educators commonly feel rewarded through their connections with other musicians and music educators. They enjoy communicating about their successes and failures, and learning through these conversations how to become better music teachers. Many music teachers also perform on the side and feel rewarded by the ability to continue making music.

Music educators also feel rewarded by their ability to impact society and the lives of their students through music, and by seeing their students grow into competent, successful musicians. Finally, music education has a long-standing tradition in the United States. Some music educators express that they feel rewarded by their ability to contribute to and carry on that tradition.

Nonmusical Work Values (How You Feel Personally or Professionally Rewarded)

In addition to the rewards they feel by helping students become better musicians, music educators feel rewarded by helping students become better overall people through music. They feel rewarded by helping other people meet their personal and professional goals, and helping students understand music for the first time. Finally, music educators feel rewarded by their contributions to society through teaching people about the arts.

Personal Characteristics

Because so much of a music educator's time is spent around people, you need to be a good people person, at least in a professional context. Many music educators express that they are introverts by nature but seem to have an extroverted teacher persona that allows them to feel comfortable around people in a professional setting.

It is also helpful if you have a great deal of patience as students of any level can be trying at times. You also need to be empathetic to your students' needs and yet be firm, fair, and consistent with the implementation of your rules and guidelines. You need to be self-confident and maintain an ability to deal calmly with potentially explosive situations. When you deal with troublesome parents, students, administrators, or other volatile situations, you also need to be a good listener, a good motivator, and a good encourager, and have a pleasant personality.

Because there are many situations that are out of your control as a teacher, you need to be flexible and be able to relate well to teachers in other areas. You also need to have a strong sense of professionalism, be willing to learn, and be self-motivated, particularly when solving unanticipated problems with schedules, parents, students, or any number of other troublesome circumstances.

SEVENTEEN
Music Librarian

As the name implies, a music librarian fulfills the same duties and responsibilities as any other professional librarian, but with a specific focus on music. Most music librarians work primarily with print and online materials including books, sheet music, research journals, professional journals, content-specific magazines, and research-based websites related to music. Other music librarians work in radio, television, or recording studios, or focus primarily on sound recordings and work more with records, CDs, and digital music files.

Currently, the music library career field is fairly well represented in music career databases and publications, yet is probably one of the lesser-known music careers to people outside the field. In addition, you will not find universities that offer undergraduate music degrees in library studies or library sciences. Even still, it is a very viable career option for musicians interested in this field.

CAREER ENTRY

As is stated earlier, there is not an undergraduate music degree devoted to music library studies. There is, however, a graduate-level degree that is usually required to become a music librarian, especially if you want to work in a college or university library. The American Library Association requires that all librarians hold a master's degree in either library or information sciences. For musicians, the appropriate master's degree is called a Master of Library Sciences (MLS) with an emphasis in music.

At the undergraduate level, you are free to choose the degree that is of greatest interest to you. It is strongly recommended that you pursue some degree in music. Either a Bachelor of Arts in Music or a liberal studies degree with an emphasis in music should adequately prepare you to pursue the MLS degree in music.

THE JOBS

The music library career field can be broken down into three broad categories. The most common type of music librarian works in a regular library setting, dealing primarily with books and other print or online musical resources. Libraries also commonly house listening collections of CDs, DVDs, and other digital recordings with which you might work.

Most music library positions are found in academic libraries in colleges and universities across the country. Only the largest public libraries, the New York Public Library for example, may have one or two music librarians on staff. In some universities, the music librarian may also be expected to teach music history, literature, or research classes in at least a part-time capacity. This is most common in universities that train students to become music librarians.

There is also some variation in the music librarian's professional responsibilities based on the type of university in which the music library is housed. In a conservatory setting, for instance, music librarians may spend a majority of their time working with scores and printed music. At research universities, on the other hand, music librarians work more with books about music, journal collections, and related research resources.

There are other professional duties that are common of all music librarians, regardless of professional setting. Most music librarians work in a public service environment, helping patrons find what they need, teaching patrons how to use the library's resources, and fulfilling related tasks at the library's front desk.

Other music librarians work mainly as catalogers. These music librarians deal less with patrons and spend more of their time working behind the scenes inventorying collections, acquiring new materials, and entering new acquisitions into the library's database. Catalogers also work with music librarians at other institutions through interlibrary loan or related programs. Primarily, a cataloger keeps the library's records in order so that patrons can find the materials they need.

Music librarians also work as archivists. Most libraries keep materials on the main library stacks for a certain amount of time. At the end of that period, the materials are moved to an archive somewhere else in the building or in a different location altogether. An archivist maintains these materials and helps patrons find resources that have been moved to the archives. Archivists also order, maintain, organize, and catalog historical materials and special collections. Archivists are also employed by large museums or the Library of Congress to manage their music holdings.

The second type of music librarian works for symphony orchestras, military performing ensembles, or other performance organizations that hold extensive collections of sheet music for their ensembles. As would be assumed, music librarians in these settings manage the collections, file music, and help the performing musicians find the parts they need for upcoming concerts. These music librarians may also mark sheet music or do other editorial work to prepare music for upcoming rehearsals. The MLS degree previously mentioned is not required for this type of music library work. It is necessary only that you have some experience in music.

Finally, music librarians can also be found in some radio stations, particularly stations like National Public Radio that broadcast mainly orchestral and operatic music. These librarians mainly catalog the sound recordings and help DJs and program hosts find the music they need for upcoming broadcasts. Because of the increasing reliance on digital media and referencing, this type of music librarian is much less common today than in prior generations.

Finally, there is a small assortment of other organizations that may hire music librarians with specific specializations. There is a well-known carillon (bell tower) in Florida, for instance, that holds an extensive collection of carillon music and hires a music librarian to manage the collection. Some music publishing companies may also hire a music librarian to manage their collection of previously published music. There is also a growing interest among private fine arts organizations in conservation or preservation of musical instruments and antiquated sheet music. Some of these organizations hire music librarians to manage their collections.

MOST PROMISING LOCATIONS

The size and type of city in which you choose to live will have a strong bearing on the type of job available to you. Because a large majority of music library positions are in colleges or universities, you need to live in close proximity to a medium to large university that is likely to have a music librarian on staff. For work as an orchestra librarian, you need to live in a large metropolitan area with an active symphony orchestra or similar performing organization. Larger cities are also more likely to have public radio stations that hire music librarians.

WHAT DOES IT TAKE TO BE A GOOD FIT IN MUSIC LIBRARY STUDIES?

Musical Skills

As a music librarian, you will need to be able to answer an incredibly diverse array of questions pertaining to all aspects of music. Therefore, you must have a strong overall knowledge of music that encompasses instrumental and vocal music, music of all time periods and genres, and performance practice. You also need to understand the basics of music theory to answer patrons' questions and help them find resources they need. You must also have at least some competence as a performer as your own performance experience and ability enables you to understand the specifications of patrons' questions and requests.

It is also common for patrons to hum, whistle, or sing a few measures of a piece they need to find, and then ask the music librarian to identify the piece and help them find the score or recording. To be successful in this task, you must have a good enough ear to recognize the melody the patron intends to find. You must also have a thorough knowledge of music history including major composers, their works, time periods, and stylistic features of each period.

Related to music history, there have been various methods of cataloging the major works of composers throughout the ages. All of J. S. Bach's music, for example, was cataloged with a BWV number, representing the *Bach-Werke-Verzeichnis* (Bach Works Catalog) system. Mozart's music was cataloged using a *Köchel* system, and therefore all titles of Mozart's music end with a K. catalog number. Because of this type of specificity in music cataloging, you must have a thorough knowledge of music publishing that encompasses the major music publishers throughout music history.

There is a final musical skill that is unique to music librarians who work for symphony orchestras or other performing organizations. Music librarians in these roles are commonly asked to prepare parts for rehearsals by marking measure numbers, temporarily omitting measures or sections of music that are not needed for a performance, or copying bowings and articulations for the string section. In this role, your knowledge of music theory must extend into performance practice of each instrument in the orchestra to mark the music appropriately.

Nonmusical Skills

As with other music careers, the most important nonmusical skill is your ability to work with people. This skill is especially important for music librarians as you will encounter people of various personalities, demographics, and other characteristics on a daily basis. You should also have a basic, working knowledge of various languages as you may frequently work with people from different countries. German, French, and Italian are particularly important to music librarians as most of the major compositions and music documents throughout history were written in one of these languages.

You should also have an extensive knowledge of the primary and secondary music research sources. In addition, music research commonly extends to art history and general history. As a result, you should have a keen ability to conduct research and find answers to miscellaneous questions.

Finally, you should have a thorough knowledge of library cataloging systems including the Dewey Decimal System and Library of Congress Classification System. Similarly, as technology has become such an integral component of research and other library systems, you should be adept at multiple facets of technology.

Musical Interests

Many librarians started out in other areas of music and were benefited in one way or another by a music librarian to the extent that they decided to become music librarians themselves. Because music librarians typically come from diverse backgrounds, they usually have a broad array of other musical and nonmusical interests.

Music librarians are interested mainly in the ability to be surrounded by music and stay connected with other musicians. Most music librarians also enjoy the schedule flexibility that allows them maintain low- to mid-level amateur performance careers or part-time careers in other aspects of music. Finally, music librarians are usually interested in the opportunity to review new music, scores, recordings, and books about music.

Nonmusical Interests

Most music librarians state that they are interested primarily in helping people find the answers to their questions. They also love the ability to share their love of music with the general public and the research opportunities that come with answering patrons' musical questions.

Music librarians in university music libraries also suggest that they enjoy the stability and security of their jobs, especially when compared to musicians in other fields. Furthermore, college music librarians suggest that being a music librarian is a great alternative career for people to stay involved in an academic setting without having to worry about the typical teaching and administrative responsibilities of being a university professor.

Music librarians are also commonly interested in the multifaceted world of literature. They enjoy working with print and online resources, and the many forms of digital and analog music recordings. Finally, music librarians are commonly interested in the applications of technology to music, research, and other library functions.

Musical Work Values (How You Feel Musically Rewarded)

Music librarians enjoy the ability to keep themselves musically involved in a number of different capacities. Many music librarians conduct their own research, perform on a part-time basis, and may also teach a class or two on the side. They feel rewarded by maintaining a certain level of involvement in each aspect of music that brings them satisfaction.

They also feel rewarded by their ability to stay immersed in music through access to recordings, books, documents, and other resources. More so, they feel gratified when they are able to share their newfound knowledge with other musicians and library patrons. They also enjoy the strong professional network among professional music librarians.

Nonmusical Work Values (How You Feel Personally or Professionally Rewarded)

The most rewarding aspect of being a music librarian is the ability to help patrons find the answers to their questions and locate the resources they need to complete a project. Many times, patrons have only a vague idea of the resources they need, and they rely on the expertise of the music librarian to identify and locate suitable resources. Music librarians suggest that their ability to help patrons offers a very tangible culmination to one's work and provides a sense of satisfaction that is not found elsewhere.

Music librarians also feel professionally satisfied by the flexibility of the daily routines that typify the life of a music librarian. A music librarian might work the front desk helping patrons find their resources one day and spend the next day opening a recent shipment of new releases. Because of this variety, music librarians suggest that there is little monotony in their daily routines.

Music librarians also feel rewarded by their ability to stay abreast of current and forthcoming publications and resources. Technological resources are also commonly available to music librarians, especially those pertaining to audio and video media. Music librarians also commonly have access to historical documents that are not available to the general public. Music librarians state that they feel rewarded by using historical documents and original source documents to make history come alive for their patrons.

Finally, music librarians feel rewarded through unraveling complex issues, answering complicated questions, and locating obscure references. They enjoy the challenge of difficult questions and sifting through layers of materials and resources in search of the correct answer. This sense of accomplishment is magnified when the process benefits another musician, librarian, or library patron.

Personal Characteristics

Just as a love of music does not always mean you are well suited for a career in music, a love of reading does not mean that you will be a good librarian or music librarian. Like any other career, there is an intricate combination of skills and other attributes that determine your fit.

First, because a large portion of your professional responsibilities involve working with the general public, you must work well with people. While this trait may seem simple, it encompasses a wide array of related attributes. Sometimes patrons can be somewhat abrupt or frustrated at their own lack of knowledge or success in the research process, and they release their frustration onto the music librarian. Therefore, you must have a great deal of patience to deal with rude or obnoxious patrons. Patience is also a vital trait as you work with patrons who have never used technology or other library resources, and rely solely on you to answer their questions.

You should also have a concern for the general public and a desire to help people locate the information or materials they need. This sometimes requires you to have a very forthcoming nature and the ability to draw people out so they can communicate their questions to you. You also need to have good speaking skills and be an excellent listener.

Next, working in a music library requires excellent organizational skills and attention to detail. Sometimes a misplaced punctuation mark or a misspelled word can result in an inaccurate research process. Having a detail-oriented personality will help you identify minute errors and locate materials for patrons in an efficient manner. Attention to detail is also vital in the intricate cataloging and numbering systems of music library catalogs and inventories.

Current libraries are also much more reliant on technology than they were in previous generations. Most libraries have replaced card catalogs with online search engines and web-based journal databases and encyclopedias. Most libraries also provide access to e-books, electronic resources, and digitized formats of other common publications. Therefore, it is helpful if you have a thorough knowledge of technology and an overall aptitude for working with technological applications pertaining to music and research.

You must also have a strong sense of tenacity, curiosity, and a knack for solving problems. Sometimes, answers to seemingly simple questions can be quite difficult to locate, and your sense of tenacity will enable you to find the answers you need. It is also quite common for library materials to be misplaced either by patrons or other librarians. Your willingness to work and ability to solve problems will help you locate lost or missing materials, just as it will help you find obscure references and answer difficult questions.

Along these lines, there are times when an answer is simply not available. While you must enjoy research and the process of finding difficult answers, you must also be able to recognize when the answer is not available. You must also be able to recognize when you may be looking

in the wrong place or need to modify your questions or research processes.

Finally, as a music librarian, you must be able to switch gears at any
given moment. Specifically, each patron's questions are usually completely unrelated to previous or future questions. Therefore, you must be
flexible and be able to mentally switch from one topic to the next with
little or no warning. Similarly, you must be able to simultaneously manage multiple projects that all compete for your attention.

EIGHTEEN

Conducting

Conductors are among the most visible of all professional musicians, particularly among performing ensembles. You see their names on the front pages of playbills and concert programs or their faces on billboards, concert promotion posters, and CDs. They signal the beginning of a concert with a ceremonial walk to the podium, bow to the audience, and downbeat of a baton. They also signal the end of a concert with a bow, a shake of the concertmaster's hand, and triumphant walk to the stage door.

Conductors are sometimes held in higher esteem than other musicians and are upheld as elite or preeminent concert performers. Many conductors are also concert soloists, are notable composers and arrangers, and have a sizable following of student conductors. They are also commonly viewed as spokespersons for their ensembles or for music as a whole.

In one sense, although conductors are among the most visible, they are among the least abundant of all professional musicians. For every major ensemble, there is only one conductor. More commonly, one conductor directs two or more ensembles, resulting in an even smaller proportion of professional conductors.

In another view, conductors are also considered one of the most common professional musicians if the term is taken in a broader sense. Just as conductors direct large professional ensembles, they also direct middle school, junior high, and high school bands, choirs, and orchestras in schools across the country. Conductors also lead student musicians in college and university ensembles, military ensembles, and community-based performing organizations.

In actuality, there are considerably more conducting jobs available in middle and high school programs than in professional ensembles. School conducting positions, however, are more accurately grouped with music education careers than conducting careers because conducting is such a small part of a music educator's job description. Therefore, if you are interested in a career in conducting, you must first consider the type of ensemble you wish to conduct and the level or age of musicians with whom you wish to work.

These factors will help you determine whether you should pursue a music education degree and career, or if you should pursue a different venue. Once you have made this determination, you may need to read one or more of the other chapters in this book that is most closely related to your career interests.

CAREER ENTRY

Because a significant portion of the careers available in conducting are located in public schools, you must have a bachelor's degree and a teaching certification to enter this career field. If you are interested in conducting college-level ensembles, it is not necessary for you to be a licensed teacher, but you usually need a graduate degree.

There is a small number of professional ensembles and performing organizations that may hire nondegreed conductors, provided that they have extensive experience and adequate training by some other means. Although these jobs may be available to nondegreed musicians, most conductors strongly recommend that you obtain a college degree before seeking employment as a conductor.

As of this writing, there are graduate degrees in instrumental and choral conducting, but there are no undergraduate degrees in conducting. Professional conductors suggest that the most suitable undergraduate degree to prepare musicians for careers as conductors is the Bachelor of Music in Music Education. Most university degree programs in music education will prepare you with the skills and knowledge that you will need to be an ensemble director, and will also adequately train you for graduate courses in conducting if you choose to continue your education.

Conductors also suggest that a degree in performance is a suitable option for students who wish to pursue careers as conductors. While performance degrees do not usually require the pedagogy classes that are required of a music education degree, they do provide extensive opportunity to participate in a larger number of ensembles than music education degrees. These ensembles may enable you to diversify your knowledge and skill set, and thereby adequately prepare you for a career in conducting.

THE JOBS

The most obvious description of the conductor's primary responsibility is to lead an ensemble in rehearsals and performances. There are a comparatively small number of professional ensembles, mainly symphony orchestras around the country that hire full-time ensemble conductors.

In a public school setting, ensemble directors may direct two or more different ensembles and also perform other teaching responsibilities, including music appreciation, music theory, or private lessons. College ensemble directors also teach conducting classes and commonly teach music appreciation, music education, or courses related to their area of expertise. A large number of college ensemble directors also write and/or arrange music for their ensembles.

There are also a variety of community ensembles in need of conductors. In these ensembles, while the ensemble members usually participate without compensation, the conductor may receive a small stipend. Conductors are also hired by each branch of the armed forces to direct the field bands, choirs, orchestras, and other military ensembles.

There are also different types of directors who are hired by professional performing organizations. An opera company or musical theatre may hire a person with a conducting background to work as a coach or rehearsal director. This conductor works directly with the performers during rehearsals but does not usually conduct performances. Performances are typically directed by the conductor of the opera orchestra or pit ensemble.

In addition to the notable college choirs, a lot of well-known choral groups are based out of large churches, indicating that conducting jobs, both choral and instrumental, are also available in places of worship. Just as the job for school ensemble directors may be more accurately described as a music educator, a conductor in a church is more of a church music director than a conductor. If you are interested in this type of information, you may need to turn to the chapter devoted to sacred music.

Finally, there are a few ensembles with particular specializations that hire conductors with specific expertise to fit the ensemble's needs. Large churches and some recording companies or publishing companies hire conductors with expertise in children's choirs. Some colleges also hire conductors with extensive music history experience to conduct collegium or early music ensembles that perform on historically accurate instruments. There are also a select number of big bands, dance bands, and other jazz ensembles where conductors are needed.

Outside the academic setting, conductors usually serve as the musical or artistic directors for the ensembles they direct. In this role, they select music for performances, organize concert schedules, and may also compose or arrange music for performances. In some ensembles, conductors also perform a number of administrative functions including hiring musicians, negotiating contracts, recruiting soloists and featured performers, managing budgets, and promoting upcoming concerts.

Many conductors are also part-time recitalists, solo performers, or composers. Some conductors perform as section members in one ensemble and conduct a different ensemble as a part-time position. It is also common for conductors to specialize in the music of a particular composer and research, write about, and perform the music of that composer as a significant portion of their performance selections.

Finally, there are some conducting opportunities in theme parks, cruise ships, or similar performance venues that employ large ensembles for live performances. Recording studios are also likely to hire conductors on a contract or as-needed basis.

MOST PROMISING LOCATIONS

As with many other music careers, the most promising location depends on the type of conducting job you want to pursue. Overall, the potential for employment is considerably higher for instrumentalists than for vocalists, so your area of expertise might have an additional bearing on potential employment. If you want to conduct in a school setting, any town or city will suffice for both instrumentalists and vocalists. For instrumentalists, there are more opportunities for wind and percussion players than string players, with the exception of large cities where school orchestras are more common.

If you want to conduct a professional ensemble, you need to live in a metropolitan area that is likely to have a number of different performing ensembles or live performance venues. Chicago, for example, houses the Chicago Symphony Orchestra, the Chicago Civic Orchestra, the Lyric Opera of Chicago, the Chicago Opera Theatre, and several other ensembles for musicians hoping to win a coveted position in the main ensembles and performing companies.

WHAT DOES IT TAKE TO BE A GOOD FIT IN CONDUCTING?

Musical Skills

Conductors set the musical and professional standards for their ensemble members, and thereby play a key role in the success or failure of the ensemble. Therefore, to be a good fit in this career field, you must exhibit a very high level of musicianship and possess a wide range of musical skills. First, if you expect high-quality performance from your ensemble members, you must be a strong performer in your primary area. Next, you must have an extensive knowledge of the performance literature for your own instrument and for the ensembles you wish to conduct.

Next, conductors are expected to read music in all clefs, meters, keys, and of all degrees of complexity. Therefore, excellent music reading and audiation skills are essential attributes of ensemble conductors. You must also have excellent baton technique and the ability to use your body, physical gestures, and facial features to communicate your musical intentions to your ensemble members.

Conductors are also expected to recognize incorrect fingerings, faulty tuning, inaccurate rhythms, poor tone, and a host of other problems. Therefore, you should have highly developed error detection skills and a keen ability to identify performers' mistakes. You should also be able to correct performers' errors in a diplomatic manner that encourages them to improve, rather than insulting or belittling them.

Next, you should have excellent theory and analysis skills. These skills are vital to help you complete the countless hours of score study and theoretical analysis of upcoming performance selections. It is also helpful if you play the piano at a proficient level as the piano is a very useful instrument in score analysis.

Finally, many conductors sing melodies, phrases, and other excerpts to their ensemble members to communicate their unique interpretation of the score. Consequently, it is helpful if you have some vocal ability and feel comfortable singing in front of other people. While you do not necessarily need to sing with the vocal quality of an opera or Broadway performer, you do need to be able to sing in tune with a decent tone and with enough confidence to communicate your intentions through your voice.

Nonmusical Skills

Like in any other music career, people skills are essential for conductors. You must also possess the leadership skills necessary to convince highly competent musicians to adopt your interpretation of a piece. This skill should be complemented by an ability to unify a group of musicians toward a singular musical goal.

You should also be proficient in a variety of languages, with a particular focus on French, Italian, and German. This is an especially vital nonmusical skill for choral conductors but is also strongly recommended for instrumentalists. Choral conductors, particularly, should at least be able to read and speak any language they wish their groups to perform.

Finally, you must be able to plan ahead, sometimes a year or more in advance. You must also be able to keep a number of tasks going at the same time and possess the organizational skills necessary to prioritize your goals and responsibilities.

Musical Interests

Most conductors state that they were led to become conductors because of their own participation in musical ensembles. Through these favorable experiences as ensemble members, they felt led to become conductors so that they could hopefully create favorable experiences for the next generation of musicians. Conductors also state that their love of music and of a variety of musical genres was a strong factor in their decision to become conductors.

Conductors are also commonly interested in being part of live performance and in the process of preparing for performances. Finally, conductors are interested in the historical and sociological aspects of music, enjoy learning about the development of music over the course of time, and enjoy discovering music's role in society throughout history.

Nonmusical Interests

Conductors are commonly interested in a wide array of areas that relate to the music their ensembles perform. These interests usually include literature, poetry, art history, and theatre. Conductors are also typically interested in playing leadership roles in ensembles and other musical organizations.

Musical Work Values (How You Feel Musically Rewarded)

Conductors are most rewarded by the ability to participate with music and the ability to lead highly skilled musicians in performances of the world's greatest music. Conductors also feel musically rewarded by helping performers understand music at a deeper level and use that understanding to improve in their ability to perform. Next, conductors feel rewarded by the ability to see how a piece changes from one performance to the next, and from one ensemble to the next.

Nonmusical Work Values (How You Feel Personally or Professionally Rewarded)

Because conductors commonly feel responsible for the success or failure of an ensemble and the overall quality of an ensemble's performances, conductors feel a sense of personal satisfaction by the ability to see tangible outcomes of hard work. Similar to school music educators and church music directors, conductors suggest that they feel rewarded by hearing improvement in a piece over time and seeing the overall progress from the first rehearsal to the performance.

Conductors also feel a sense of personal satisfaction by learning how people learn and using that information to become better conductors. Through their own experiences in front of their ensembles, conductors enjoy learning how to become better at what they do and in turn help their ensemble members become better themselves. They also become better equipped to influence ensemble and audience members by their increased effectiveness as conductors.

Personal Characteristics

Conductors frequently work with musicians whose talent has not yet developed, who speak a different language, who did not practice their part, or who exhibit other behaviors that may become frustrating, both to the conductor and to the ensemble members. Consequently, you must be a patient person to be a good fit in conducting. Your patience will enable you to keep yourself in check and to defuse potentially volatile situations among ensemble members during rehearsals.

Second, you must be an effective communicator and be able to communicate well with a variety of people and personalities. As a conductor, you must be able to communicate verbally to articulate your musical interpretation and other objectives to your ensemble members. You must also be able to communicate nonverbally through baton movement, physical gestures, and facial expressions, again, to express your musical interpretation to your ensembles and help them understand your musical intentions.

Next, you must be well disciplined, dependable, and stable. Because you will work with musicians of various personalities, you must have a strong sense of leadership and be able to deal with temperamental dispositions. You may also occasionally receive poor reviews from music critics, patrons, or other reviewers who may not agree with your interpretation, selection of music, or other aspects of your performances. Therefore, you must be thick skinned and able to deal well with criticism.

Finally, as you may work as an accountant, business manager, concert promoter, or fulfill other administrative roles as an ensemble conductor, you must be very well organized. You must be able to manage multiple tasks and keep up with numerous deadlines, concert schedules, and related events. You must also be musically organized in the sense that you may need to have five or more scores in various stages of preparation at any given moment.

NINETEEN

Instrument Repair

As long as there have been instruments, there has been a need for people with the skills, tools, and patience to repair them. Whether undertaking a summer overhaul of an entire high school band instrument inventory or meticulously soldering a custom lead pipe on the instrument of a concert virtuoso, repair technicians enable musicians to continue teaching and performing by ensuring their instruments are in premium condition. Instrument repair is an in-demand field for musicians, with an ever-expanding array of expertise and opportunity.

CAREER ENTRY

As of this writing, there is no bachelor's degree in instrument repair. Furthermore, while many colleges may offer one or two classes in instrument repair, there are only three colleges that offer an instrument repair certificate, and this certificate is only available for winds and percussion. The most commonly recommended means of career entry for instrument repair is through an apprenticeship with a master technician. Apprenticeships usually last one to two years and may be found in large repair shops and with independent contractors willing to take an apprentice.

For pianists, there is a formal certification to become a Registered Piano Technician that is offered through the Piano Technicians Guild. Like other instruments, however, you prepare for this certification through a formal apprenticeship with a registered technician rather than a college preparatory program.

If you choose to pursue a college degree, there are three options that are most highly recommended by repair technicians. First, you have to know the instruments you intend to repair, so a degree in performance may serve you well. Second, if you plan to repair band instruments, you will work primarily with school band programs. Therefore, to help you learn your customer base, a degree in music education may be beneficial. Finally, many instrument repair technicians manage their own shops or eventually manage a music retail store. If this is your long-term goal, a degree in merchandising or music business may be a good option.

THE JOBS

Repair technicians are most commonly found in music retail shops. Technicians in commercial or retail music stores generally repair a wide range of instruments and contract with local schools, churches, or performing organizations. Sometimes, technicians begin their careers in a retail shop and eventually start their own repair business once they have established a reputation with enough clients, completed their apprenticeship, and have enough of their own resources. Some larger colleges and universities and performing arts facilities also hire in-house technicians to repair school instruments and sometimes teach instrument repair courses.

Technicians are also hired by instrument manufacturers to make and repair instruments. These technicians are usually more specialized, working only with one type of instrument. These technicians may also work directly with virtuoso performers to customize instruments to the performer's specifications. Manufacturers also hire technicians to research means of improving the quality of current products and generating new products.

There are four broad categories of instrument repair, each with its own areas of specialization. First, band repair technicians work with woodwind, brass, and percussion instruments. Some technicians aspire to work in large shops and therefore are trained to work in bulk, work quickly, and repair all types of band instruments. Other technicians specialize in one instrument family and sometimes even in one specific instrument.

In the second category are a group of specialists called *luthiers*, or technicians who build and repair stringed instruments. In this category, some technicians specialize in guitars and other folk instruments. Others specialize in orchestral strings (violin, viola, cello, bass, and harp) or one particular type of orchestral string instrument.

The next category includes people who manufacture, tune, and repair pianos. Due to the size, weight, and delicate nature of this instrument, there are some piano technicians who offer piano moving services in addition to the more common tuning and maintenance services. This is the only repair field whose technicians spend a larger portion of their time tuning instruments and the only field to require certification for membership in the professional organization (Piano Technicians Guild). Once you complete an extensive apprenticeship and pass the required proficiencies and exams, you receive the Registered Piano Technician endorsement.

The final category of repair technicians is much less formalized and standardized than the previous three. With the advent of electronic and digital instruments, a new group of repair technicians is needed who are skilled in this field. In truth, most musicians who play these types of instruments train themselves to do their own repair work and sometimes build their own instruments. However, there is still a need for musicians to repair electric guitars, basses, keyboards, drum machines, and related instruments. These technicians also commonly repair sound systems, public address (PA) systems, speakers, and other equipment needed for electronic and digital music.

Finally, there are also part-time career options available in instrument repair. Most instrument repair technicians are full-time technicians. There are also a lot of technicians who maintain part-time jobs as performers or maintain part-time private lessons studios. Some technicians also begin to accumulate large inventories of their own instruments and sell used instruments on the side. Finally, there are a small number of technicians who eventually begin to manufacture their own brand of instruments.

MOST PROMISING LOCATIONS

The most promising locations for instrument repair depend on the type of instruments you want to repair and the type of job you would like to have. The primary factor for consideration is the population density of the area in which you wish to live. Specifically, there should be enough musicians of the type of instruments you wish to repair to provide a viable income. You should most likely be willing to live in a midsize to large city or be willing to cover a lot of territory in smaller communities and rural areas.

WHAT DOES IT TAKE TO BE A GOOD FIT IN INSTRUMENT REPAIR?

Musical Skills

You must first be a good performer on the instruments you intend to repair. You should know the entire range of each instrument's capabilities, limitations, tendencies, alternate fingerings, and other traits. Specifically, you need to be a good enough performer to know how each instrument should respond and sound, and recognize when some part of an instrument is not working properly. You must also have a very good ear to hear the subtle nuances of an instrument's tone to diagnose and repair a variety of instrumental malfunctions.

Nonmusical Skills

First, you must be able to work well with all kinds of people. Instrument repair technicians consistently interact with ensemble directors, performers, delivery personnel, other technicians, and a general customer clientele. In addition to your ability to repair instruments in a timely manner, your people skills will be a significant factor in your customers' evaluation of your work and whether they will return to you or seek a different repair technician for future work.

You must also possess a mechanical aptitude and be able to work well with your hands. This skill requires a certain hand-eye coordination and physical dexterity that not everyone possesses. This aptitude is also commonly coupled with an aptitude for problem solving and the ability to systematically identify why an instrument is not functioning as it should.

Musical Interests

Instrument repair technicians suggest that this is a great career field for musicians who want to stay involved with students but are interested neither in music education nor in performance. Technicians are commonly interested in serving young musicians and doing their part to help musicians become successful. They are also interested in the ability to stay active as performing musicians, at least on a part-time basis.

Nonmusical Interests

Repair technicians are interested in the mechanics of instruments and other devices. They enjoy learning how things work, the common causes of malfunctions, and how to fix the problems they encounter. They are interested in tasks that involve working with their hands and the tools that help them find solutions to their problems. Some technicians are also interested in the business aspect of the industry, particularly technicians who plan to manage their own store or retail shop.

Musical Work Values (How You Feel Musically Rewarded)

Instrument repair technicians feel musically rewarded by the ability to play a key role in ensuring that a young musician has a future. A beginning musician with a faulty instrument does not possess the skills or experience to know that the instrument is malfunctioning. Instead, he or she may feel that his or her lack of talent is the reason for poor sounds, faulty intonation, or other problems. This frustration may lead the student to pursue other nonmusical interests. When the instrument is in good condition, however, there is a stronger likelihood that the student will persist in his or her musical endeavors.

Repair technicians also feel rewarded by the diversity of musical challenges with which they are presented on a daily basis. They enjoy the process of figuring out why an instrument is not working and what they can do to restore an instrument to proper working condition. They also feel rewarded by the ability to contribute to the success of a performance.

Nonmusical Work Values (How You Feel Personally or Professionally Rewarded)

Repair technicians feel a sense of pride by seeing immediate results. They feel rewarded by the ability to see tangible outcomes of their work and the sense of gratitude that performers express when their instruments have been repaired. Technicians also feel rewarded when performing musicians speak highly of them, contributing to a positive reputation in the professional community.

Finally, repair technicians enjoy the lifelong friendships that are formed with performers, customers, and clients over the years. And, like most other professional musicians, technicians feel rewarded by the ability to support themselves in a job that they enjoy.

Personal Characteristics

The process of diagnosing and repairing an instrument is usually a very tedious task. In some cases, you may spend an entire day fine-tuning a singular aspect of an instrument. Other times, there may be a simple task that must be repeated multiple times on a large inventory of instruments. In either case, repair technicians must exhibit a great deal of patience, self-drive, and motivation. It is also helpful if you are able to sit for extended periods of time and maintain focus on a single task. Also, as an instrument repair technician, you must have a good eye for detail and the ability to spot the most insignificant malfunction on an instrument.

Once a malfunction is located, the process of repairing it may involve extensive trial and error. Therefore, you should be very persistent and tenacious and have an aptitude for creative problem solving. This process also requires that you be willing to learn new ways to repair instruments or find innovative solutions to unusual problems.

Instrument repair also requires that you have a positive attitude as you may commonly deal with frustrated musicians or experience your own frustration when solutions do not come quickly. You must also be able to receive criticism from customers who are not satisfied with your work and learn from customers' critiques rather than interpret their comments as a personal assault.

Also, depending on the type of instrument you wish to repair, it may be helpful if you have considerable upper body strength. While this may not be as important for a piccolo or a trumpet, repairing pianos or sousa-phones requires the need to lift heavy objects.

Finally, you must have a genuine concern for the customer that drives you to produce high-quality work. According to repair technicians, the idea is not to make an instrument functional, but to make it work like new. Mediocre work on a student's instrument may result in the student's continued frustration and could result in the loss of his or her love of music. A professional musician, on the other hand, will recognize the mediocre work and will keep coming back until the repair is completed satisfactorily.

Annotated Bibliography

This bibliography inventories a number of common career books and websites, and provides a general description of the contents of each resource. The contents have been arranged in the following three categories:

1. Music career books

   a. General
   b. Specific to music business/industry
   c. Specific to performance

2. Career websites

   a. General
   b. Specific to music
   c. Additional online resources

3. General career inventories and career advising books

In each category, resources have been listed alphabetically by the author's last name. Due to the consistently changing nature of music careers, this list only includes resources that have been published since 1990. Finally, the inclusion or unintentional omission of any resource in this bibliography is intended neither as an endorsement nor as a critique. The resources have only been listed as a reference for additional information.

MUSIC CAREER BOOKS

General

Bohonos, Kate, and Evonne Tvardek, eds. *Exploring Careers in Music* (2nd ed.). Reston, VA: MENC: National Association for Music Education, 2000.

In 1990, the American Music Conference combined efforts with the National Association for Music Education (MENC, which is now NAfME) under the direction of Bjorneberg to update a 1976 text, *Careers in Music*. The second edition of this text, entitled *Exploring Careers in Music*, was published by MENC in 2000 (Bohonos and Tvardek). According to the authors, career inventories and descriptions were created through consultations with representatives from professional organizations related to each career included in the text. The 2000 edition categorizes music careers into the following fields: Music Education, Music Performance, Music Business, Music Communications, the Recording Industry, Music Technology, and Other Music Careers (v–vi). For each career description, the authors include specific places or types of employment, suggestions for career entry, and preparation, skills, and abilities. For most careers, musical and nonmusical skills and abilities are listed. A brief statement indicating the professional organization that was consulted concludes each chapter.

Field, Shelly. *Career Opportunities in the Music Industry* (6th ed.). New York: Checkmark Books, 2009.

Career Opportunities in the Music Industry was first published in 1986 and has since undergone five revisions. For this text, Field compiled information on over eighty music careers and inventoried these careers into twelve overall categories. In the 2009 text, the description of each career is divided into two parts: the first part presents a list in a bulleted format and the second part presents the same information in narrative form with an explanation of the content. For each of the careers discussed, Field includes the following information: "alternate titles, career ladder, position description, salary ranges, employment prospects, advancement prospects, education and training, experience, skills, personality traits, best geographical location, unions and associations, and tips for entry."

In the position description section, the author provides a general description of the typical job-related responsibilities associated with each career. Each chapter discusses job variations among employers based on the company's size, location, or organization. Each chapter also includes a statement describing how the function of each job affects or interacts with the other positions in the company. The final section, describing each career, provides recommendations and suggestions concerning common resources for job postings and for entering the industry. Concluding the text, Field includes nine appendixes providing supplemental information in a compiled format. Appendixes include names of colleges offering music degrees, music unions and professional organizations, record companies, music agents, publishers, and copyright agencies. A bibliography and index follow the appendixes. The bibliography provides names and references of various print and online resources related to the multiple career fields.

Gerardi, Robert. *Opportunities in Music Careers*. Chicago: VGM Career Books, 2002.

Gerardi's *Opportunities in Music Careers* opens with an introduction to the music industry and includes descriptions of careers in the music industry. Gerardi's first chapter is devoted to general career advice including writing cover letters, getting a business card, making demos, and performing solo recitals. The remaining chapters define and describe various music careers. Gerardi also includes information about unions and professional organizations, where orchestral performers find jobs, and how aspiring musicians supplement their incomes while taking auditions. Gerardi's text concludes with a bibliography of books on various careers pertaining to music and the music industry.

Goldberg, Jan. *Great Jobs for Music Majors* (2nd ed.). Chicago: VGM Career Books, 2005.

The first chapters of Goldberg's *Great Jobs for Music Majors* describe general practices of career advising as they apply to music students. In the remaining chapters of this book, the author describes seven career categories, detailing a total of thirty-seven music careers. Although there is a general emphasis on performing careers, a number of business-related careers are also included. Each career description concludes with a section in which one or two noted professionals are introduced and asked to describe how they entered and succeeded in their specific field of the music industry.

Music Business/Industry

Baskerville, David. *Music Business Handbook and Career Guide* (9th ed.). Thousand Oaks, CA: SAGE, 2009.

Baskerville's *Music Business Handbook and Career Guide* was first published in 1978 and has been periodically revised. In this text, Baskerville introduces several music careers and provides a description of each. A final chapter in Baskerville's text is devoted to general considerations for those interested in pursuing a career in music. This section includes such information as the importance of a good résumé, successful interviewing, and other elements commonly discussed by career advisors.

Crouch, Tanja J. *100 Careers in the Music Business* (2nd ed.). New York: Barron's Books, 2008.

Crouch's *100 Careers in the Music Business* is written specifically for students interested in the business-oriented careers in the music industry. Crouch organizes the book into fifteen chapters that represent career categories for musicians. Each chapter is further divided into the various careers in each field. Crouch interviewed musicians from each career field and includes excerpts from interview transcripts to provide information for each career. Crouch also includes success stories of the interviewed musicians and suggestions for career entry. For each field,

Crouch defines job titles and the position of each career on the specific career ladder of the related industry. The author also specifies how jobs differ in title and function based on the size of the company. Finally, Crouch defines the different types of jobs in each field.

Des Pres, Josquin, and Mark Landsman. *Creative Careers in Music* (2nd ed.). New York: Allworth Press, 2004.

Whereas Crouch's text is intended for people interested in the business aspects of the music industry, Des Pres and Landsman's book is intended for people who want to pursue creative, artistic, or performing careers in music business. In *Creative Careers in Music*, Des Pres and Landsman describe a unique selection of music careers that may or may not exist in other professional pursuits. According to the authors, the book is meant for performers in "mainstream commercial popular music industry . . . [specifically] recording, broadcast, music publishing and the concert business" (vi) and may therefore be inapplicable to teachers, orchestral players, or opera performers (vi). It is further clarified that the book's contents are most relevant for "players, singers, composers . . . songwriters . . . producers and engineers" (vii).

Johnson, Jeff. *Careers for Music Lovers and Other Tuneful Types* (2nd ed.). New York: McGraw-Hill, 2004.

The opening sentence of *Careers for Music Lovers and Other Tuneful Types* states: "Since Thomas Edison first put recorded music on a cylinder . . . young people around the world have dreamt of being part of the excitement of the music business where it is still possible to become a star practically overnight" (ix). This statement is included in the introduction of Johnson's text to specify that the book is written for musicians aspiring to enter the recording industry. Specifically, the author states that the purpose of the book is to discuss the many types of careers and popular performers that comprise the music industry. Johnson begins each chapter with an introduction describing the overall purpose or function of the specific career discussed in the chapter. The remaining section of each chapter includes a written transcript of interviews with professionals in each field. Although some interviews vary, most include the following questions: "How did you break into the business?" (2); "What skills and/ or education does one need to make it [in your field]?" (7); "What do you like most about your job?" (8); "What is the most challenging aspect of your job?" (8); "What advice would you give someone who wants to get into [your field]?" (8), "Why does the record company need [your job]?" (21); and "How did you get into [your specific job within the industry]?" (32).

Performance

Beeching, Angela Myles. *Beyond Talent: Creating a Successful Career in Music* (2nd ed.). New York: Oxford University Press, 2010.

In the preface of *Beyond Talent: Creating a Successful Career in Music,* Beeching specifies that *Beyond Talent* is written for specifically for performers but contains information that may be applicable to musicians in all music career fields. When *Beyond Talent: Creating a Successful Career in Music* was first published, Beeching was a music career counselor and director of the New England Conservatory Career Services Center. Beeching has since left this position and is currently an independent music career consultant (www.angelabeeching.com).

In the first several chapters, the author provides a series of tips and suggestions for entry and success in a music career. The second part of Beeching's book is devoted to the identification and description of music careers. Following this discussion, Beeching provides a second categorization of music careers that is reserved for those musicians who perform on a part-time basis and supplement their income with nonperformance endeavors. In the final pages of *Beyond Talent: Creating a Successful Career in Music,* Beeching provides an inventory of music careers for performers, educators, administrators, and other venues.

Cutler, David. *The Savvy Musician: Building a Career, Earning a Living, and Making a Difference.* Pittsburgh: Helius Press, 2010.

One of the newer music career texts on the market, this book focuses on the importance of entrepreneurialism for a new generation of performing musicians. More directly, Cutler's text discusses at length many of the skills in addition to music that will enable a rising performer to establish him or herself as a musician, and maintain a fulfilling career. These skills include business, creating a marketable product, utilizing online resources, dealing with the press, recording technology, people skills, freelancing, finance, and performance skills. Four appendixes conclude the text and describe additional resources and strategies for aspiring performing musicians.

The Savvy Musician is supplemented by a companion website (http://savvymusician.com) that provides additional online resources, a blog, and presentations by the author. David Cutler is a professional composer, arranger, and performer currently teaches at Duquesne University where he serves as the director of entrepreneurship studies.

Uscher, Nancy. (1990). *Your Own Way in Music*. New York: St. Martin's Press, 1990.

This book is written as a career guide for performing musicians. It contains four main sections:

- Getting Your Skills Together: A resource guide for the professional performer (1), this section discusses résumé writing, finding and preparing for auditions, getting a professional head shot, finding grants, and other related information.
- Support for the Musician: This section discusses organizations and foundations that provide monetary support for the arts and artists (63).
- Making Your Way in the World: This section discusses the professional mind-set of determination that must be upheld by the professional musician, especially during the process of taking auditions (103).
- The fourth section lists and discusses career options for professional musicians. Uscher interviewed musicians and includes their life stories as depictions of the various careers. Uscher also researched and reports the success stories and financial wealth of other musicians and incorporates those accounts into the text.

CAREER WEBSITES

General

America's Career InfoNet. Accessed July, 26, 2012. www.careerinfonet. org.

America's Career InfoNet is a web-based career advising center sponsored by the US Department of Labor. As of this writing, the site offers many of the typical services found in a traditional career advising office including occupation inventories, advice on interviewing, writing a résumé, and other related services. Occupations are listed in order of relevance to the field of interest as indicated by the website user. For each career listing, the website delineates "occupation description, state and national wages, state and national trends, knowledge, skills and abilities, and tasks and activities" required for entry and tenure in the chosen occupation. "Tools and technology, education and training, related occupations [and] web resources" are also included in the career descriptions (America's Career InfoNet, 2012, Occupation Profile [Music] Directors and Composers). With the exception of state-specific employment trends and salaries, all career descriptions are directly excerpted from the online version of the *Occupational Information Network*.

Discover. Accessed July 20, 2012. https://actapps.act.org/eDISCOVER.

As of this writing, access to the Discover website requires a user login and may not be accessible to the general public. The Discover program was organized by the American College Testing Program as an online career advising resource offering many of the same services provided through traditional career counseling services. As of this writing, the website (https://actapps.act.org/eDISCOVER) provides access to "career databases, majors, schools, job postings, inventories [and a site for creating a] personal portfolio" (Discover, 2012, Main Menu).

For each career listed in its career inventory, the site provides the following information: "work tasks and settings, qualities, training and education, salary outlook, likes and dislikes, related occupations, and [resources for] more information" (Discover, 2012, Musician [Instrumental]). Items listed in the "qualities" section include music and nonmusical skills, and a brief inventory of personal traits. Each career listing also provides the DOT number, Occupational Information Network number, US Department of Education Career Cluster, and Guide to Occupational Exploration number. The Career Cluster and Occupational Exploration numbers are additional career classification systems, much like *OOH* and *O*Net*, used by career advisors.

Occupational Outlook Handbook. "Occupational Outlook Handbook Online." Accessed July 29, 2012. www.bls.gov/OOH.

Commonly called the OOH, this website is an online version of the most recent of JIST's career publications based on information provided by the US Department of Labor. Although the content concerning career descriptions is similar to that of the *O*Net DOT* (see the following), the OOH includes additional introductory information to assist in the career advising process. Specifically, the authors of the OOH include a three-page, 120-item personality inventory based on the research of John Holland.

Specific to Music

CareersinMusic.com. Accessed July, 29, 2012. www.careersinmusic.com.

The Career Jobs link includes a primary listing of approximately twenty music career options with a basic overview of each career. Although music business careers are the primary focus of the website, careers in music education, composition, music therapy, and performance have also been included on the inventory. In the description of each career, the author has included estimated salary expectations, personal qualifications, recommended skills, knowledge, required training, and prior experiences for career entry.

National Association for Music Education. "NAfME Career Center." Accessed July 6, 2012. musiced.nafme.org/careers.

The National Association for Music Education (NAfME) maintains a Career Center link on its website. On this page, NAfME inventories and describes a variety of music careers in thirteen categories. The website also contains a printable Careers in Music brochure that provides a general overview of each career and requisite knowledge, skills, and training.

Additional Online Resources

Network of Music Career Development Officers (NETMCDO). Accessed June 16, 2012. www.musiccareernetwork.org.

According to the authors, "The Network of Music Career Development Officers (NETMCDO) is an active international group of professionals working in the area of music career development" (http://www.musiccareernetwork.org/, 2012).

This organization was founded by Nancy Beeching, author of *Beyond Talent: Creating a Successful Career in Music*. NETMCDO membership is open to anyone with an interest in music career advising. Most of the members are university music faculty members and professional musicians. The group meets annually and maintains an ongoing e-mail LISTSERV for members to discuss research, publications, and current events related to music and music career advising.

Many university music departments, particularly in large universities and conservatory settings, sponsor their own music career websites. In some cases, the website is specific to the music degrees offered by the individual university. Most websites, however, provide a general description of a wide array of music careers.

Sample university music career websites include the following:

- Berklee College of Music: www.berklee.edu/careers/
- Texas State University: www.music.txstate.edu/resources/career-development/musiccareers.html
- University of North Carolina Wilmington: http://uncw.edu/career/music.html

General Career Inventories and Career Advising Books

Farr, Michael (dir.). *O*Net Dictionary of Occupational Titles* (4th ed.). Indianapolis: JIST Works, 2007.

Occupational Outlook Handbook. Indianapolis: JIST Works. 2010.

JIST Works produces two major career resource publications, both based on information provided by the US Department of Labor: the *O*Net DOT* (Farr 2007) and the *OOH* (2010). The *DOT* is a record of approximately 1,100 careers and information about the included occupations and is available online and in print. According to Farr (2007), the current edition of the *DOT* replaces previous editions, boasting more than 12,000 career descriptions. Farr indicates that many of the careers described in prior editions either employed too few people or were too focused to be considered viable career options, and were therefore eliminated from inclusion in the current edition (2007). The six music careers listed in the current edition are (1) music arrangers and orchestrators, (2) music directors, (3) composers, (4) musical instrument repairers and tuners, (5) musicians and singers, and (6) instrumental musicians (Farr, 2007).

Each career listed in the *DOT* is categorized by a Standard Occupational Classification (SOC) system and is given a corresponding universal number. This number is used by career advisors to reference specific careers in any one of the publications using the SOC system. For each career discussed, a number of characteristics are described. These characteristics include education and training, number of people employed, annual earnings, occupational description, personality type, skills and abilities, general work activities, physical work conditions, other job characteristics, [and] related jobs, among others (Farr, 2004).

Gordon, Virginia N. *Career Advising: An Academic Advisor's Guide*. San Francisco: Jossey-Bass, 2006.

Gordon's *Career Advising* text stands apart from other resources included in this bibliography as it does not inventory careers or provide descriptions of careers or career fields. Rather, as implied by the title, this book is intended to be a guidebook for career advisors. The text describes general career advising principles and procedures, and discusses the justifications for these practices. The book was written in cooperation with the National Academic Advising Association.

VGM Career Encyclopedia (5th ed.). Chicago: McGraw-Hill, 2002.

VGM has published many books related to careers and career advising. Their publication *Career Encyclopedia* (2002) lists approximately 200 careers and includes two career options for musicians. For each career included, the editors describe "the job, places of employment and working conditions, qualifications, education and training, potential and advancement, income [and] additional sources of information" (263).

About the Author

Eric Branscome is assistant professor of music and coordinator of music education at Austin Peay State University in Clarksville, Tennessee, where he teaches undergraduate and graduate courses in music education and supervises music student teachers.

Dr. Branscome is the author of *Essential Listening Activities* (2008), *Essential Rhythm Activities* (2008), and *Music Board Game Workshop* (2011). His other publications and research interests include elementary music curriculum development, early childhood music, music teacher education, and music career advising. Dr. Branscome lives in Clarksville, Tennessee, with his wife, Devyn, and two daughters, Hope and Meg.